Barbara Ellis, Editor

Frances Tenenbaum, Series Editor

HOUGHTON MIFFLIN COMPANY
Boston • New York   1998

Soil and Composting

The complete guide to building healthy, fertile soil

NANCY J. ONDRA

For information about permission to reproduce selections from this book,
write to Permissions, Houghton Mifflin Company, 215 Park Avenue South,
New York, New York 10003.

Taylor's Guide is a registered trademark of Houghton Mifflin Company.

Library of Congress Cataloging-in-Publication Data

Ondra, Nancy J.
      Soil and composting : the complete guide to building healthy, fertile soil / Nancy Ondra.
            p.   cm. — (Taylor's weekend gardening guides)
      Includes index.
      ISBN 0-395-86294-9
      1. Garden soils. 2. Soil management. 3. Organic gardening. 4. Compost. I. Title. II.
      Series.
      S596.75.O54   1998
      635'.0489 — dc21   97–46590
                                                                                    CIP

Printed in the United States of America.

WCT 10 9 8 7 6 5 4 3 2 1

Book design by Deborah Fillion
Drawings by Elayne Sears
Cover photograph © by Karen Bussolini / Positive Images

CONTENTS

Healthy gardens start with healthy soil. Most home gardens aren't blessed with great soil to start with, but the good news is it's possible to improve almost any site—you just need the know-how to choose the right tools and techniques for the job. This book is your guide to building rich, productive soil, which will provide all your plants with everything they need for lush leafy growth, beautiful flowers, and flavor-packed vegetables. You'll also learn how mulching, making compost, and fertilizing play essential roles in creating a bountiful garden.

Any time is the right time for starting to improve your soil. Whether it's covering bare soil with compost over winter, adding organic matter in spring, fertilizing in summer, or planting cover crops in fall, you'll find that your soil-building efforts pay off in better garden growth than you ever thought possible.

Bumper vegetable harvests start with good soil preparation and care. A garden design like this, with prepared beds separated by paths, concentrates your soil-building efforts where the plants will grow. Covering pathways with straw, sawdust, or other slow-to-rot material helps control weeds.

CHAPTER 1
UNDERSTANDING YOUR SOIL

Creating great garden soil isn't a big one-time chore, it's an ongoing process. While preparing a new garden bed presents an obvious opportunity to improve the soil, every time you dig, plant, or cultivate you have a chance to enhance your soil's structure, drainage, and fertility. Just keeping it mulched with organic matter, such as compost or shredded bark, helps improve it.

But before you can decide how to improve your soil, you need to know what you are starting with. That's because the natural characteristics of soil in general—and those of your soil in particular—will influence how you care for it. Soil type also plays a major role in determining which plants will grow and thrive in your garden with a minimum of care.

This chapter presents essential information about soil and its composition along with techniques for evaluating your soil. As you learn, it's smart to keep a notebook with observations and test results for future reference. You'll also want to keep notes of the soil improvement steps you take so you can see whether they

Installing raised beds is often the easiest way to solve a variety of soil problems, including heavy clay soil, compacted conditions, or a poorly drained site. This garden features a wood-sided raised bed planted with strawberries and a rock-edged bed for a mix of perennials and herbs.

lead to increased fertility or improved drainage, for example. Keeping a record also helps you make educated decisions about future garden care, such as when and how much to mulch or fertilize.

WHAT IS SOIL?

Soil is the layer of transition between the rock core of the earth and the thin web of life on its surface. This thin layer, measured in inches or feet, is a complex and dynamic mixture of several components, including rock and mineral particles, organic matter, water, air, and, in healthy soil at least, a vast quantity of living organisms. Surprisingly, "ideal" garden soil isn't solid: it is actually about half pore space, with roughly 50 percent of the pores filled with air and 50 percent with water. Approximately 45 percent of soil is mineral particles, and 5 percent is organic material. In real garden soil, the relative proportions of these components will vary, depending on the season, the weather, and the region you live in. They also vary at different depths in any one location. For instance, the upper soil layer (commonly called topsoil) is typically much higher in organic matter than lower "subsoil" layers.

Minerals. Soil is composed primarily of broken-down rock. These mineral particles are divided into four different categories based on their size. The coarsest particles are still recognizable as stones and gravel, but the primary particles are sand, silt, and clay. Sand particles, which range in size from 2 millimeters down to 0.5 millimeters, are smaller than gravel but can be seen with the unaided eye. Silt particles are smaller than sand, between 0.5 and 0.002 millimeter, and can be seen only with the aid of a microscope. Clay particles—those less than 0.002 millimeter across—are so fine they can be seen only with an electron microscope. Although the different sizes of these particles may not seem significant, each kind plays a unique role in determining many important soil traits, including texture, fertility, and drainage. (See "Soil Texture" on page 10 for more on the influence of particle size.)

Organic Matter and Humus. "Organic matter" is a catchall term for both living organisms and plant and animal residues in various stages of decomposition.

Most gardens don't have great soil to begin with; it has to be built. Mulching with organic matter prevents wind and water erosion and also adds essential organic matter to the soil. Mulched paths direct traffic, thus minimizing soil compaction in the beds.

Healthy soil is teeming with tiny organisms that gradually digest leaves, stems, roots, and other debris, breaking them down into unidentifiable crumbs. As these organisms die, they are in turn digested by those that remain. In the process, essential nutrients such as nitrogen, phosphorus, and sulfur are released from complex molecules and transformed into simple ions that plants can absorb through their roots. The breakdown of organic matter also produces sulfuric, carbonic, and nitric acids, which help dissolve rock and release the minerals that plants need to grow well. This process makes it clear why soil that is rich in organic matter is fertile.

As soil organisms feed on and break down debris, the volume of organic residue decreases greatly. Eventually, all that is left is humus, a complex, concentrated molecular stew that is characteristically dark brown or black. As the end product of decomposition, humus is relatively resistant to further breakdown.

But while it won't contribute much more to the soil by releasing nutrients, humus plays an important role in fertile soil by holding large amounts of water and dissolved nutrients—even more than clay particles can hold. Both organic matter and humus are also important in improving the physical condition, or structure, of the soil because they cause particles to clump together, creating pore space for air and water. That's why regular additions of compost, chopped leaves, and other forms of organic matter make garden soil easier to dig. Besides making your work more pleasurable, loose soil is easy for plant roots to grow through, and it allows water to soak in faster and more deeply, encouraging extensive root growth. (See "Soil Structure" on page 13 for more on this important aspect of soil.)

Water and Air. The spaces, or pores, between soil particles can be filled with water or with air—and the roots of most plants need both to grow well. Some plants—bog plants are an obvious example—are much more tolerant than others of "wet feet," a condition in which most or all of the soil pores are filled with water, but most plants need balanced amounts of water and air in the soil. When

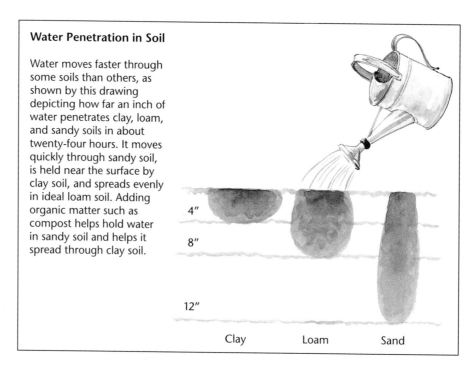

Water Penetration in Soil

Water moves faster through some soils than others, as shown by this drawing depicting how far an inch of water penetrates clay, loam, and sandy soils in about twenty-four hours. It moves quickly through sandy soil, is held near the surface by clay soil, and spreads evenly in ideal loam soil. Adding organic matter such as compost helps hold water in sandy soil and helps it spread through clay soil.

4"

8"

12"

Clay   Loam   Sand

precipitation or irrigation wets the soil, water runs down through the larger spaces, which fill with air, but clings to the smaller ones. Gravity pulls water down, while adhesion—the tendency of water to stick to a surface—slows its movement. That's why sandy soils, which have many coarse particles and large pore spaces, tend to drain quickly. Clay soils, on the other hand, have tiny particles that fit together closely, leaving only tiny pores that hold water tightly. In fact, this adhesion may be so strong that roots cannot pull in the water they need, so they may wilt or die even though the soil still holds moisture. Medium-size pores hold some water, but loosely enough to allow the excess to drain and roots to draw up what they need.

Unlike the mineral and organic components of soil, which are fairly stable, the water and air contents are always changing. After rain or irrigation stops, water continues to move through the soil for hours or days. Ideally, the upper soil layers will hold some water in medium-size pores while letting the excess drain down through the larger pore spaces. Eventually it reaches the water table, unless its flow is impeded by a change in soil texture or structure (such as a dense clay layer or a compacted zone). Draining water will also slow down when it reaches a transition zone between finer and coarser soils—regardless of which lies above the other—and collect in the soil immediately above that zone.

To grow the widest range of plants, it's best to keep your soil relatively loose and free-draining.

LIFE IN THE SOIL

Soil not only supports life, it contains life. A huge and diverse population of organisms, ranging from microscopic bacteria to plump, wriggling worms, is at home in healthy soil. Many of these organisms play an important beneficial role in maintaining soil and plant health by recycling nutrients, mixing particles, and improving soil structure.

Soil Microorganisms. Healthy soil teems with microorganisms. Most numerous are bacteria, so small they're barely visible with a microscope. Most bacteria occur in clumps or colonies in contact with organic residues or plant roots. While some kinds of bacteria cause plant diseases by attacking tissues and interfering with normal growth, other kinds are beneficial. Many, for instance, aid in the process of breaking down organic matter into humus. A few kinds of bacteria also perform chemical conversions that are useful to plants. Some bacteria transform atmospheric nitrogen, a gas that plants can't use, into nitrates, a nutrient that plants need for growth and can readily absorb.

Soil fungi produce tangled masses of threadlike filaments called mycelia, which weave among the soil particles. Like bacteria, the fungi that live in the soil can be harmful or beneficial. Those that feed on living tissues are the ones that can cause disease problems such as rots and wilts. But many kinds of fungi feed only on dead material: these play a vital role in decomposing organic debris in the soil.

Most microorganisms are clustered in the soil zone closest to plant roots, and they interact with the plant's growth processes. Soil microorganisms give off compounds that can either stimulate or inhibit root growth. Some "good guys," for instance, act as a shield to defend plants from attack by harmful organisms. Plant roots, in turn, may release substances that are beneficial to the microorganisms. One example of such a partnership is mycorrhiza, a special interaction between certain plant roots and soil fungi. The threadlike fungal mycelia extend the surface area of the roots, spreading many inches beyond the roots to collect nutrients (especially phosphorus), which are then shared with the plant. In turn, the plant provides sugar—an energy source—to the fungus. These kinds of relationships are very common in nature. Other beneficial microorganisms attack and help control disease-causing microorganisms and nematodes, or roundworms.

Regular additions of organic matter in the form of compost, chopped leaves, grass clippings, and other garden debris go a long way toward building the populations of beneficial bacteria and fungi in your soil. If disease-causing microorganisms do get the upper hand, you may need to grow different plants in that part of your garden, at least for a few years. When the microorganisms don't have any susceptible plants to feed on, they will eventually starve and die off, giving the beneficials a chance to take over again. This technique, called crop rotation, is especially useful in the vegetable garden, where growing the same crops in the same place each year can quickly allow disease organisms to build up.

Earthworms and Other Animals. Many kinds of earthworms are found in all types of soils, wherever there is moisture and enough organic matter for them to

Take an Earthworm Count

Most soil organisms are tiny, so it's hard to get a good idea of how biologically active your soil is. One way to get a rough idea, however, is to count the number of earthworms in your garden. The more worms you find, the more likely it is that beneficial microorganisms are prolific as well. Remember that earthworms tend to burrow deep in the soil during very cold, hot, or dry weather, so you'll get the most accurate results if you try this test in mid- to late spring or early to mid-fall, when the soil is relatively warm and moist.

To take an earthworm count, mark a 1-foot square on the soil in some part of your garden. Then dig out that area to a depth of 6 inches, and place all the soil in a big bucket or tub. Sift through the soil with your fingers and count the number of earthworms you find. If you find ten worms or more, that's a good sign. If you come across fewer than that, you may need to make an extra effort to add organic matter to the soil. Ample amounts of food will encourage earthworms and other beneficial organisms to multiply.

feed on. The more organic matter in your soil, the more earthworms you'll have. They are most active near the surface, but they can burrow several feet deep, especially during cold or dry weather. Their vertical burrowing carries and mixes material up and down through the soil. Their burrows also provide channels for air and water to travel through the soil.

Other small animals in the soil include nematodes, millipedes, centipedes, pill bugs, snails, spiders, ants, and many other kinds of insects. Individually, these organisms are small, but collectively they have a great effect on the makeup of your soil. They feed on living and dead plant parts, on bacteria and fungi, and on each other. Like earthworms, these organisms help mix the soil as they tunnel up and down and laterally, opening passageways that enhance air and water infiltration in the process. A few soil-dwellers, such as root-attacking nematodes and grubs, are pests, but the vast majority have a beneficial impact on your garden. Adding organic matter helps to encourage some of the beneficials, as does leaving some undisturbed areas (such as ground cover plantings or mulched areas) where these creatures are protected from frequent digging or tilling.

SOIL TEXTURE

As rocks break down into smaller and smaller pieces, they turn into soil particles—sand, silt, and clay. The relative percentages of these different-size particles
determine your soil's texture, fertility, drainage, and need for irrigation.

- **Sand.** Wet or dry, sandy soil is a pleasure to dig and till, and it is easy
  for plant roots to grow through. However, water (with its dissolved nutrients) and air pass readily through the large pores between sand particles,
  so sandy soil dries out quickly after a rain and doesn't hold a large reser-
  voir of water or nutrients.
- **Silt.** When silty soil is very dry, water beads up and runs off the surface
  rather than penetrating. But once it is moist, it absorbs and retains more
  water and nutrients than does sandy soil.
- **Clay.** When dry, clay tends to shrink and crack apart, and it hardens into
  dense, bricklike clods. While it is slow to absorb moisture, clay soil holds
  water (and the nutrients dissolved in it) tightly once it soaks in. For this
  reason, soil high in clay tends to get waterlogged during rainy spells.

Of course, few soils are pure sand or silt or clay. To describe soils of different
textures, soil scientists have come up with "textural classes" based on the relative
percentages of the three different-size particles. A soil with moderate amounts of
all three sizes is referred to as loam. Loamy soils are considered ideal for gardening because they are easy to dig and effective in retaining water and nutrients.

There are several ways to assess your soil's texture. You can do a few simple
tests right out in the garden, or bring a sample indoors for more detailed testing.
While texture may vary from one site to another, a single sample from a property of an acre or less in size will give you a good idea of your soil's overall texture. If you have a very large property, you may want to test a few samples from
different areas and note the results on a sketch map, marking where you collected
the samples and how they tested.

Testing Texture by Feel. A simple way to get a rough estimate of your soil's texture is to dig up a trowelful of moist soil. First try rubbing a bit of the soil
between your thumb and forefinger. Sandy soil has a coarse, grainy, gritty feel.
Silty soil has a slippery feel, like talcum powder, while clay feels sticky.

Now take a handful of the soil, squeeze it, and open your hand. Sandy soil will crumble apart right away; soil with more silt and clay will stay in a lump. If the lump falls apart when you tap it lightly, your soil is in the loam range. If you can mold the soil lump with your fingers, it's high in clay.

The Jar Test. For a more precise evaluation, collect a trowelful of soil from a few inches below the surface. Remove any pebbles, debris, leaves, or roots, and break up any lumps. Put a cupful of soil and a cup or two of water in a clear glass jar. (A narrow, upright jar is better than a short, wide one.) Cap the jar tightly, then shake it vigorously until all the soil is suspended in the water. Set the jar on a table where you can leave it undisturbed for a full day.

After about one minute, the largest particles will have settled to the bottom. Use a ruler to measure and record the depth of that layer, which is the sand. After about an hour, the intermediate-size particles—the silt—will have settled out. Measure the depth of the settled soil again, then subtract the amount that was sand to determine the depth of the silt layer. After about twenty-four hours, measure again and subtract the amounts of sand and silt to get the depth of the clay layer.

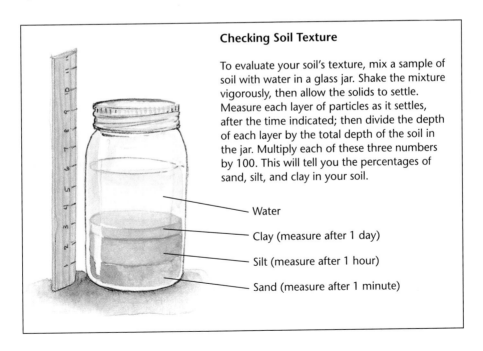

Checking Soil Texture

To evaluate your soil's texture, mix a sample of soil with water in a glass jar. Shake the mixture vigorously, then allow the solids to settle. Measure each layer of particles as it settles, after the time indicated; then divide the depth of each layer by the total depth of the soil in the jar. Multiply each of these three numbers by 100. This will tell you the percentages of sand, silt, and clay in your soil.

Water

Clay (measure after 1 day)

Silt (measure after 1 hour)

Sand (measure after 1 minute)

What Class Are You In?

After doing the jar test, locate the sand, silt, and clay percentages you found on the sides of this USDA Textural Triangle. Then find the point where the three lines meet. Knowing the textural class of your soil will help you make effective decisions about plant selection, fertilizing, and watering.

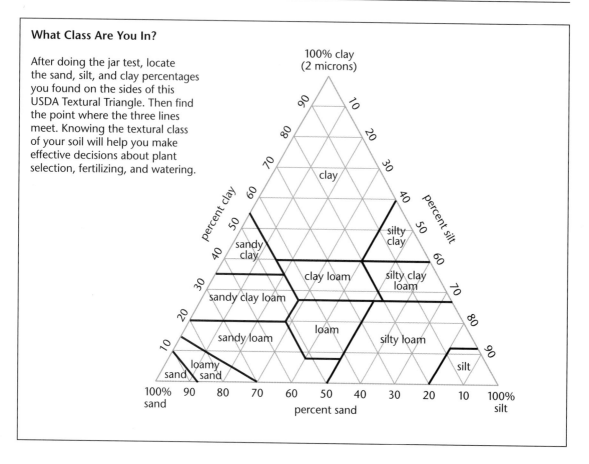

To calculate the percentages of sand, silt, and clay, divide the depth of each layer by the total depth of settled soil, then multiply by 100. For example, if the sand layer is ½ inch deep and the soil totals 3 inches deep, you'd divide ½ by 3 (result 0.17) then multiply by 100 to get the percentage (17 percent sand). Repeat the same process to get the percentages of silt and clay.

Loam, the "ideal" garden soil, can vary considerably in its makeup. As a group, loamy soils contain less than 52 percent sand, between 28 and 50 percent silt, and 7 to 27 percent clay. But if your soil falls outside these ranges, don't despair. Although it isn't practical to try to change soil texture by adding sand or clay, there are plenty of tricks to make the best of what you have: see "Heavy Clay Soil" on page 31 or "Light, Sandy Soil" on page 35 for suggestions.

SOIL STRUCTURE

The way in which individual soil particles clump together, or aggregate, is referred to as soil structure. Among other things, sizes and shapes of these aggregates influence the way water and air move through it. That's because structure determines the sizes of the soil pores.

Some soils have no structure. Some may be so tightly packed that they are nearly impossible to dig; in others the particles may not hold together at all. But the two types of structure you're most likely to find in garden soil are "blocky" and "granular." Blocky structure is common in subsoil layers, which have been somewhat compressed by the topsoil layer. If your surface soil has this type of structure, it's likely that the topsoil has been stripped away in the past. The smaller the blocks, the easier it is for roots to penetrate and for water to drain down through the soil. Large blocks tend to hinder downward root growth and cause water to collect in the surface soil.

Ideal garden soil has a loose granular or crumblike structure. This kind of structure is found especially in soil that is high in organic matter, because soil organisms release sticky materials that promote the formation of soil aggregrates as they decompose organic debris.

Soil structure can change over time, for better and for worse. Alternate cycles of freezing and thawing or wetting and drying tend to clump particles together.

Common Soil Structures

Soil with granular structure, which is ideal for gardening, breaks into small crumbs when worked. It provides ideal conditions for good root growth. If your soil tends to form rough cubes or blocks when you break it apart, it needs some improvement; adding organic matter will help make it more granular and will help maintain that structure.

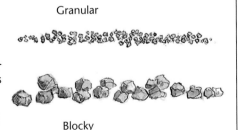

Granular

Blocky

Humus compounds released from organic residues help to bind the mineral particles, thereby stabilizing the aggregates. Fine roots, such as those of grasses, also play a major role in binding soil into desirable clumps. These naturally formed aggregates contribute to good soil structure.

On the down side, aggregates can melt, collapse, or break apart if you disturb your soil when it is wet. Even a heavy rain is enough to destroy the structure of exposed surface soil, forming a puddle that creates a crust as it dries. When aggregates break down into individual particles, the soil gets compacted, and it becomes more difficult not only for air and water to penetrate but for roots to penetrate as well. Walking on garden soil or running heavy equipment over it also destroys aggregrates, compressing the pore spaces in the process. Aggregates of clay soil are particularly vulnerable to disturbance, so it is important not to till or cultivate clay soil when it is wet. Protecting soil with mulch or ground covers also helps maintain good structure.

Determining Your Soil's Structure. This test is an easy one: simply take a handful of moist surface soil and lightly crumble it around in your hand. If the soil falls apart into rounded crumbs, it has a granular structure. If it tends to stay in larger lumps, try breaking the lumps apart with your fingers. Soil with a blocky structure breaks into cubes that may have sharp or somewhat rounded edges.

Soil that is well aggregated—meaning that it crushes easily but will hold together if pressed—is said to be friable or to have good tilth. Either term means that the soil is easy to dig or till and is ideal for root growth. By adding compost, leaf mold, and other types of organic matter, you can improve your soil's structure.

SOIL FERTILITY

Green plants need at least sixteen different elements for growth: carbon, hydrogen, oxygen, nitrogen, phosphorus, sulfur, potassium, calcium, magnesium, iron, manganese, zinc, copper, molybdenum, boron, and chlorine. Plants obtain the first three—carbon, hydrogen, and oxygen—from carbon dioxide in the air and from water. All the rest are absorbed from the soil. These elements are called nutrients, and soil rich in nutrients is called fertile soil.

The sand and silt particles in your soil contain most of the plant nutrients as part of their structure, and they release these nutrients very, very slowly as the particles decompose. Although clay particles contain few nutrients, they do play a major role in soil fertility by providing plenty of surface area for water and its dissolved nutrients to cling to. Organic matter is also a key factor in fertility. Besides holding on to water and dissolved nutrients, it also provides nearly all of the nitrogen and most of the phosphorus and sulfur that plants receive.

Few gardeners are blessed with soil that naturally has just the right balance of nutrients for best plant growth. And even if a nutrient is present in your soil, it may not be in a form that plants can use. Plants need iron, for instance, but they can't absorb iron oxide (rust), which is one of the most common forms of iron in the soil. Interactions among different nutrients can also limit availability. If your soil is high in calcium, for example, plants may have difficulty absorbing potassium and magnesium. Nutrient availability also changes at different levels of alkalinity or acidity (pH).

Fortunately, plants have a remarkable ability to extract nutrients from soil. Different plants require different amounts and proportions of the essential nutrients, but many garden plants grow well in soil of average fertility. So a little time spent evaluating your soil's current fertility and adding organic matter and fertilizers to correct any imbalances really pays big dividends in the form of more vigorous plants and a more beautiful garden. (For information on choosing and applying plant nutrients, see "Applying Fertilizers" on page 77.)

Testing Your Soil's Fertility. The most reliable way to determine fertility is to test a sample at home or send it to a laboratory. Most garden centers and garden supply catalogs sell at least one brand of home soil-test kit at a relatively low cost. Most of these tests use indicator dyes, which change color under different conditions, and provide color charts for interpreting the results.

On a per-test basis, home test kits cost about the same as most state testing services but less than most private labs. Testing labs, however, send a detailed report on the availability of major nutrients in your soil. Most will also recommend how much fertilizer and other amendments to add to improve your soil for the plants you want to grow. (Ask for organic recommendations when sending in your sample.) In general, home tests are less accurate than laboratory results. But if you home-test repeatedly, you will soon become more adept at doing the tests and reading and interpreting the results.

Whichever type of test you choose, the first test serves as a baseline appraisal of your soil. By repeating the tests every year or two you can monitor the effects of the treatments you use. Keep notes on the test results, the materials you add, and how your plants look and grow, and in time you'll develop the eye of an experienced gardener.

With either a home or a lab test, it's essential to collect a representative soil sample to get meaningful results. Dig a hole a few inches deep and collect a spoonful or two of soil from the side of the hole. Repeat the sampling in ten or so spots around your garden and mix all the soil together to get one representative sample. To compare different parts of your yard (a new, unimproved bed against an established garden, for instance), collect samples from each area and keep them separate. Be sure to label which is which.

SOIL pH

Soil pH is a measure of its acidity or alkalinity. It has an important effect on the vigor and health of plants, because it determines which nutrients can dissolve in

Collecting a Soil Sample

To collect a soil sample for testing, remove grass, leaves, and any other organic matter from the soil surface and dig a hole 3 to 4 inches deep. Collect a spoonful or two of soil from the side of the hole. To obtain a representative sample for an entire garden, collect and mix soil from several locations.

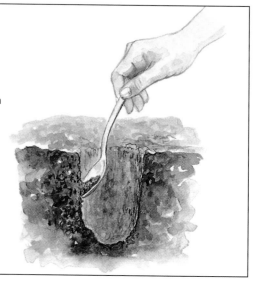

Soil-Testing Labs

Cooperative Extension Service offices across the country offer inexpensive soil-testing services. Contact your local office to find out how to obtain a soil-testing kit. In some states, kits can be purchased at garden centers or local libraries. The following companies offer soil testing by mail.

I.F.M.
333 Ohme Garden Road
Wenatchee, WA 98801

Peaceful Valley Farm Supply
P.O. Box 2209
Grass Valley, CA 95945

LaRamie Soils Service
P.O. Box 255
Laramie, WY 82070

Symo-Life Inc.
RD 1, Box 102
Gap, PA 17527

the soil water and thus be available to them. It also influences the activity of organisms that live in the soil.

Understanding Soil pH. The acidity or alkalinity of soil is closely related to soil water. Each molecule of water is made up of two hydrogen atoms and one oxygen atom. Normally, these atoms cling together tightly, but substances in the soil can cause water molecules to come apart or ionize, forming hydrogen ions and hydroxyl ions. The relative proportions of hydrogen and hydroxyl ions determine the acidity or alkalinity of the soil solution (the soil water and everything dissolved in it). If there are more hydrogen ions than hydroxyl ions in the solution, the soil is said to be *acid*. If hydroxyl ions outnumber hydrogen ions, the solution is *alkaline* (or basic). If the numbers of hydrogen and hydroxyl ions are the same, the solution is *neutral*.

Although the effects of these two ions are great, their actual numbers are very small. To make communication easier, scientists use a system called the pH scale to rate acidity and alkalinity. The whole scale runs from 0 to 14. At pH 7, the midpoint, which indicates neutral pH, there are equal numbers of hydrogen and hydroxyl ions. As the pH numbers decrease from 7 to 0, the concentration of hydrogen ions increases, meaning the solution is more acid. As the numbers

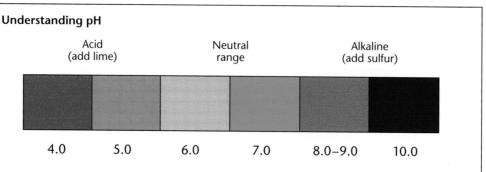

Understanding pH

Acid (add lime)		Neutral range		Alkaline (add sulfur)	
4.0	5.0	6.0	7.0	8.0–9.0	10.0

The pH scale is a measure of acidity and alkalinity. Most plants thrive in soil that is slightly acid to neutral (6.5 to 7.0). If your soil is more acid than 6.5 or more alkaline than 7.0, you can add lime or sulfur to adjust the pH or you can choose plants that are naturally adapted to your soil's existing pH.

increase from 7 to 14, the concentration of hydroxyl ions increases, meaning the solution is more alkaline. Each number on the scale differs from the preceding one by a factor of 10. That means that a pH of 5 is 10 times as acid as a pH of 6, and a pH of 4 is 100 times as acid as a pH of 6.

Soil pH typically ranges from about 4 to 8, although it can be higher or lower, depending on where you live and how your soil has been treated in the past. Regions of high rainfall tend to have acid soil, for instance, while regions with dry climates tend to have alkaline soil. In general, a pH range near neutral (roughly 6.5 to 7.0) is considered ideal for most garden plants. Within this range, most nutrients are available in forms that plants can use. In soil that is more acid or more alkaline, some nutrients join with others to form compounds that will not dissolve in water, making them unavailable to plants.

If the pH of your soil is outside of the ideal range for the plants you want to grow, you have two options: either add lime or sulfur to adjust the pH or revise your plant choices to include those that are adapted to your soil's natural pH. For more information on these options, see "Acid Soil" on page 37 and "Alkaline Soil" on page 40.

Determining Soil pH. Because a soil's pH is closely related to its nutrient content, it makes sense to test for both characteristics at the same time. Most home soil-test kits include a pH test, and most soil-testing labs routinely report pH. If

Checking for Contamination

The soil around buildings or near roads or driveways may be contaminated with debris, concrete, oil, salt, or lead. To check for possible problems on your property, look for buried trash that was abandoned after construction or renovation projects. Remove any chunks of concrete or plaster, since these release lime into the adjacent soil. Also check near driveways and parking areas for oil-stained soil (which you'll need to dig up and remove). If you use rock salt for deicing sidewalks and driveways during the winter, there's a good chance the salt-laden runoff water has drained into nearby planting areas. Sometimes you'll see a white crust of dried salt on the soil; in other cases, you may just notice that plants grow poorly in these areas. If you suspect a problem, consider having your soil tested for salt by a soil-testing lab. For tips on handling "salty" sites, see "Saline or Sodic Soil" on page 43.

Lead contamination can be a problem in some areas. Lead occurs naturally in all soils, normally at very low levels. Lead in the soil usually doesn't harm plants, but it may accumulate in their roots and leaves.

And lead is poisonous to humans, causing blood and kidney problems in adults and affecting the brain and nervous system in children.

In urban areas, automotive exhaust is the main source of lead pollution, although the rate of contamination has declined considerably in recent years, because most vehicles have switched to unleaded gasoline. But lead levels may still be quite high in the soil adjacent to busy streets and freeways. Another source of lead pollution is lead-based paints, used in the past and still found on many older buildings. When the paint flakes or is scraped off, chips land on the ground near the foundation. The chips break down into dust, releasing lead into the soil. Before growing food plants close to a busy street or an old painted building, have the soil tested for lead. (Your local Cooperative Extension Service or county health department can give you the name of a lead-testing lab in your area.) If your soil sample tests positive for lead, use that site only for flowers and other ornamental plants. Do not eat vegetables grown in lead-contaminated soil.

you wish to test only for pH, buy a home pH test kit through a garden center or garden supply catalog. With either a home or a lab test, it's important to collect a representative sample from the area you want to evaluate, as explained in "Testing Your Soil's Fertility" on page 15.

SOIL DRAINAGE

Your soil may have an ideal balance of nutrients, but if there is too much or too little water, your plants won't be able to take in what they need, and their growth will suffer. That's why it's important to evaluate your drainage and, if necessary, take steps to improve it. While poor structure can mean that the soil drains too quickly or too slowly, keep in mind that the site also plays a role.

Plant roots need water, of course, but they also need oxygen, which they get from air in the soil pores. If your soil is waterlogged (meaning that all its pores are filled with water), your plants suffer. If deprived of oxygen, roots—and thereby the whole plant—will eventually suffocate. It may take days or weeks for a plant to drown, but at the same time other problems are going on. For instance, bacteria in waterlogged soil give off hydrogen sulfide, a gas that is poisonous to roots. And dead roots are vulnerable to infection by fungi, which can proceed into living tissues and kill off an already weakened plant.

Plants vary in their ability to withstand wet soil. Bog and aquatic plants are specially adapted to these conditions; other species that normally grow in well-drained soil tolerate occasional immersion in water, such as that caused by spring

Testing Soil Drainage

Test soil drainage when your soil is moist but not soggy. First, remove the top and bottom from a large metal can and dig a hole about 4 inches deep and wide enough to hold the can. Push the can into the hole so that the bottom rim is firmly against the base of the hole and the upper rim extends a bit above the soil surface. Fill the can to the top rim with water. An hour later, use a ruler to measure how much the water level has dropped. A drop of at least 2 inches indicates that the soil will provide adequate drainage for most plants. If the water level has dropped less than that, the drainage is poor.

For best growth, most vegetable crops need soil that remains evenly moist but not wet. Here cabbage and other crops grow in mounded beds, which ensure good drainage. Mulched pathways hold in soil moisture.

flooding. Other plants demand perfect drainage to survive. A soil with moderate to good drainage allows you to grow the widest range of flowers, vegetables, shrubs, and trees. You may choose to improve the drainage in soggy spots by installing drains or building up the soil in raised beds. Or you may decide to grow moisture-loving plants in those areas. For more information on coping strategies, see "Wet Soil" on page 47.

In some instances a soil may drain *too* well, meaning that water and dissolved nutrients quickly move beyond the reach of plant roots. This is likely to be a problem only in very sandy or gravelly soil. For tips on improving the moisture-holding capacity of fast-draining soils, see "Light, Sandy Soil" on page 35. Sloping sites can also be very dry, if water runs off faster than it can soak in; see "Sloping Sites" on page 50 for suggestions.

Testing Drainage. You can learn a lot about your soil's drainage by watching the flow of water during and after a heavy rainfall. Note areas where water runs off quickly, as well as low spots where water collects.

CHAPTER 2
IMPROVING YOUR SOIL

If your soil is less than perfect, don't despair; you're not alone. Get a group of gardeners together, and you're sure to hear plenty of complaints about rocks, impossible-to-dig clays, and tough, dry spots where it seems nothing will grow. But you'll also hear success stories about how determined gardeners have overcome their problem soils. With a little know-how, you too can build healthy, fertile soil and grow a great-looking garden on just about any site. This chapter provides that know-how, along with coping strategies for a variety of problematic soil conditions, from dealing with heavy clay soil to coping with very acid or wet sites.

Building great soil is really a rather simple process, although not a labor-free one. First, get in the habit of regularly adding compost or other kinds of organic matter to create and maintain good soil structure. And as you're building a loose, crumbly structure, help keep it that way by working your soil at the right time, when it is neither too wet nor too dry.

Vegetables, flowers, or herbs will thrive in the light, fluffy soil in these raised beds. The mulch in the paths—newspapers topped with leaves—will decompose by season's end. After that it can be raked up onto the beds to add organic matter to the soil.

If you do nothing else for your soil, keep it covered with a layer of organic mulch such as shredded bark or chopped leaves. Mulch protects the soil from erosion and compaction, keeps it cool and moist, and adds organic matter.

ADDING ORGANIC MATTER

Most soils naturally contain roughly 3 to 5 percent organic matter. Even this small amount offers great benefits to plants, releasing needed nitrogen and other nutrients as it is decomposed by soil organisms. But this miracle material can do much more. Digging or tilling compost, chopped leaves, grass clippings, and other forms of organic matter into garden beds can help loosen up tight clay soil, making it easier for roots to penetrate and for water to drain through. In loose, sandy soils, organic matter helps the particles cling together and hold more water and nutrients. Regularly adding organic matter to any soil provides food for a wide range of soil organisms, thus keeping the soil biologically healthy and making plants less susceptible to harmful soil fungi and bacteria.

The only way to get an accurate assessment of your soil's organic content is to find a soil-testing lab that will evaluate organic matter (see "Soil-Testing Labs" on page 17 for a list). It's probably not worth having your soil tested just for this, but if you can get this test done at the same time as pH and nutrient tests, the results can be helpful. Testing every few years helps you fine-tune decisions on how much organic matter to add each year.

Many gardeners never bother to have their soil's organic content evaluated; they just routinely add compost or other organic materials each year. One of the great things about organic matter is that it's pretty hard to add too much. In warm climates, in fact, it's nearly impossible to overdo it, as soil organisms work fast in warm conditions, and they'll quickly break down whatever you give them.

The different forms of organic matter all have desirable effects, so choosing among them is a matter of price, availability, and convenience.

Compost. Composting home garden debris and kitchen scraps is a great way to create your own free soil amendment. For information on making and using this gardener's gold, see chapter 5, "Making and Using Compost." If you need more compost than you can create at home, or if you need it in a hurry, consider buying locally produced compost. Many municipalities, for example, now make and sell (or give away) compost from collected lawn clippings, tree leaves, and chipped brush. Some towns also sell composted sewage sludge, usually a dark, granular substance that bears little trace of its origins.

Work homemade or purchased compost into new beds before planting, or spread it around existing plantings and top it with a more uniform, attractive mulch, such as shredded bark or chopped leaves. "Using Compost" on page 92 offers more details on when and how much compost to apply for best results in different areas of your garden.

TIPS FOR SUCCESS

RECYCLE LEAVES AND TRIMMINGS

It's possible to add organic matter to the soil—and save yourself some work, too—by simply not clearing away spent foliage in some parts of the landscape each year. This technique isn't effective for every site, but it works well in areas covered with ground covers or mass plantings of perennials such as daylilies or hostas. The foliage simply decomposes in place, returning organic matter to the soil. Be sure to remove and destroy any diseased foliage, however.

Chopping up garden trimmings in place rather than taking them to the compost pile is also effective. When cutting back spent flower stems of irises or daylilies, for example, use your pruners to cut them into inch-long pieces and let them fall right onto the soil around the plant. That saves hauling the trimmings to another area and returns nutrients right to the bed. This easy technique is also best used in less visible areas. Again, be sure to remove and destroy any disease-infected plant parts.

Agricultural and Processing By-Products. Another possible source of organic matter is recycled waste products, such as bedding and manures from cattle, poultry, or horse farms; processing wastes from canneries; spent mushroom compost; and hulls from grain mills or chocolate factories. The materials available depend on the industries common in your area. You might need to drive a pickup truck to the source (or have the material delivered by an independent contractor), but chances are the price will be low. If you have a choice between fresh and aged material, take the older, darker stuff. It will have a more immediate beneficial effect on soil structure. If only fresh material is available, use it as a mulch or layer it in a compost pile for a season before adding it to the soil.

Sawdust and Bark Chips. Sawdust and bark chips are cheap and abundant in some parts of the country. Fresh or coarse wood chips should decompose for several months before they are added to the soil. The microorganisms that decompose wood need nitrogen to do the job, and they can "steal" nitrogen that would otherwise be available to plants. Adding a nitrogen source when applying wood-based amendments helps speed the breakdown without depriving plants of the nitrogen they need. Scatter about 2 pounds of blood meal over each 1-inch-deep layer of wood chips spread over 100 square feet. Wait until the chips have turned dark, soft, and crumbly before mixing them into the soil.

Peat Products. Peat is basically compost that forms naturally in wet areas. Most peat comes from sphagnum moss, a coarse-textured moss that grows in shallow freshwater bogs throughout the northern United States, Canada, and Europe. Old, dark, dead, compressed sphagnum moss is called peat moss, sphagnum peat, or simply peat. Peat moss is sold under several brand names in bags or bales or in bulk.

Reed-sedge peat is also collected from natural deposits of decomposed reeds, sedges, cattails, and similar marsh plants. When relatively young, reed-sedge peat is coarse-textured, with lots of visible stems. It breaks down quickly into a fine-textured, dense, humusy muck. Reed-sedge peat is generally much less expensive than sphagnum peat.

Keep in mind that all forms of sphagnum moss and peat are acid and may affect your soil's pH. And while they hold generous quantities of moisture once

How Much Do You Need?

To get plantings off to the best possible start when preparing the soil in a new garden bed, you can add as much as 25 percent organic matter. That means spreading a 3-inch layer of material on the surface and working the bed 12 inches deep (to mix 9 inches of soil with the 3 inches of amendment). This works out to roughly 1 cubic yard of amendment per 100 square feet of bed.

In addition to giving your plants an excellent start, adding this much organic matter and thoroughly working it into the soil will also make a big difference in how your soil feels and how easily it is worked.

When preparing existing beds for replanting, you won't need to add as much organic matter or dig as deeply. Working a 1- to 2-inch layer of material into the top 6 to 8 inches will go a long way toward keeping your soil's organic content high.

wet, they can form a water-repelling crust on the soil when dry. In most cases, compost is a better soil amendment. Save peat products for loosening the soil where you want to grow acid-loving plants, such as azaleas, rhododendrons, and blueberries. And always work sphagnum moss or peat into the soil—never use it as a mulch.

WORKING SOIL AT THE RIGHT TIME

Although you can dig in your garden pretty much any time of year that the soil isn't frozen, if you are adding a lot of organic matter or other amendments to the soil, do so at least a few months before planting. This gives the bacteria, fungi, and other organisms a chance to break down the amendments and release the nutrients into forms plants can use.

Whenever you dig or till, it's vital to check the soil's moisture content before lifting a shovel or starting up the tiller—to protect yourself as well as your soil. Digging dry soil is backbreaking work, and tilling it can break soil crumbs into a powdery dust. Working with wet soil can be tough on the back, too, and if the soil is high in clay, you'll be left with rock-hard clods when it finally dries. Either way, you can quickly destroy the good soil structure you've spent years developing.

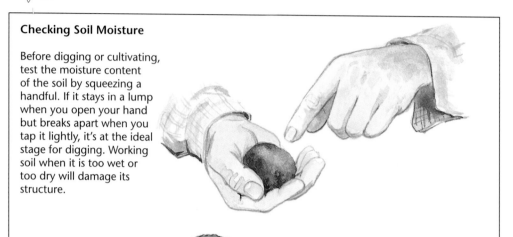

Checking Soil Moisture

Before digging or cultivating, test the moisture content of the soil by squeezing a handful. If it stays in a lump when you open your hand but breaks apart when you tap it lightly, it's at the ideal stage for digging. Working soil when it is too wet or too dry will damage its structure.

To quickly check moisture content, squeeze a handful of soil from the site before digging or tilling. If it makes a ball that holds together tightly after you open your hand, it is too wet. Wait a day or so and check again. If the soil is dust-dry, give the site a good soaking, then test again the next day. Ideally, the soil should hold together when you first open your hand but crumble easily when you tap it with a finger.

SETTING PRIORITIES FOR SOIL IMPROVEMENT

In a new garden, soil improvement may seem like a huge, tiresome job. Fortunately, it's not necessary to prepare all parts of your garden to the same extent. Focus your efforts on the areas where they will have the most effect, then work on other areas as you have time. Here are some pointers to help you plan your soil-building priorities.

Top Priority: Annual and Vegetable Beds. These plants have fine roots that are too weak to penetrate hard soil. They look best and are most productive when pampered with the best possible soil conditions.

Once you have prepared your soil, avoid walking or sitting on it when planting or tending the garden. Even light foot traffic can compact soil, reducing the pore space available for essential air and water.

Buying Soil for Your Garden

If you are trying to prepare a very difficult site, the easiest and fastest way to begin may be to buy large quantities of topsoil or soil blends to fill beds and prepare planting areas. Keep in mind, though, that buying topsoil can be an iffy business. You may get an unwelcome crop of weeds as well as stones and debris, and the soil itself may be less than top quality. Ask neighbors or fellow gardeners in your area about their soil-buying experiences, and see what suppliers they recommend. Before buying a truckload, ask the supplier where the soil is from. If possible, you might even want to visit the collection site to see for yourself what you are buying.

Soil blends (frequently called improved soil) are usually more expensive than plain topsoil, but they are a worthwhile investment for small areas such as flower beds. Depending on what part of the country you live in, the soil blend might include composted tree leaves, sawdust, bark chips, manure, and other organic materials. Call local nurseries and landscape contractors and ask if they sell truckloads of improved soil. The price will depend on the mixture and the quantity you buy.

With either plain topsoil or improved soil, plan on applying at least a 4-inch layer (and preferably 6 inches or more, especially for perennials) over the whole planting area.

Second Priority: Perennials, Lawns, and Ground Covers. Once established, these plantings last for years, so it's worth putting some effort into digging deep, loosening compacted subsoil, and adding plenty of organic matter to their soil. Given deep, loose, well-drained, fertile soil, perennials survive much better through winter cold and summer heat and drought.

Leave Trees and Shrubs until Last. Most trees and shrubs grow best when planted in native (unamended) soil. Nurseries used to recommend adding peat moss or compost to the soil when planting, but in recent years researchers have observed that trees planted in fluffed-up soil do not spread their roots out beyond the hole. This limits the availability of water and makes them less stable in high winds. If you have plenty of time and energy and want to create a shrub border or other large planting, you might want to improve the soil over the whole area so that each plant has room to spread its roots. For single specimens, however, it's generally best to leave the soil unamended.

GROWING YOUR OWN SOIL AMENDMENTS

One time-tested way to improve just about any soil before planting a garden is to devote a season or two to growing green manures, sometimes called cover crops. These plants cover the soil, protecting it from wind and water erosion, and enrich it by supplying organic matter, much as animal manures do. When cut down and dug or tilled into the soil, they decompose and provide energy to soil organisms, produce acids that dissolve mineral nutrients from the soil, and increase the amount of humus in the soil. In addition to being used before a garden is ever planted, green manures can be used to improve the soil in an established garden. They are especially useful in the vegetable garden, where they can be incorporated into a program of crop rotation — see "Vegetables" on page 103 for more information.

Green manures work best for soil building in warm, humid climates. In dry climates, irrigation is usually needed to produce a useful amount of top growth. And in cool climates, green manures take longer to decompose after they are worked into the soil, so crop planting may be delayed by several weeks until they have worked their magic.

Choosing a Green Manure. There are several options for good green manures. Grains are popular with home gardeners. Rye, wheat, and barley are usually sown in the fall and turned under in spring, while oats are sown in spring and turned under in summer. These plants all make a dense stand of grassy foliage aboveground and a soil-binding mass of roots underground. Buckwheat, a broad-leaved grain, is one of the fastest-growing green manures, but it needs warm temperatures to germinate. Sown in early summer, it can grow 2 to 3 feet tall and be ready to be turned under within ten weeks.

Several legumes, including alfalfa, sweet clover, cowpeas, and vetch, are also useful as green manures. The roots of legumes are colonized by bacteria that convert nitrogen from the air into a form that plants can use. When you turn a legume cover crop under, some of that nitrogen is available for the next planting.

Planting and Managing Green Manure Crops. To plant a green manure, till or dig the soil as you would for regular planting, then rake the surface smooth. To ensure an even stand, divide the recommended quantity of seed (2 to 4 pounds per 1,000 square feet for grain crops, or 1 to 2 pounds for legumes) in half. Sow half as you walk back and forth from north to south and the other half as you walk from east to west. Then use the flat side of a rake or a wide board to press the seeds into the soil, and water regularly to get the seedlings off to a good start.

It is usually best to turn under the crop just before it begins to bloom. (Don't allow green manures to set seed or you'll have a garden bed full of weeds next season.) The top growth is tender at that stage and decomposes most quickly. If the cover crop has grown dense and tall, you may need to mow it down. Then dig or till the bed to mix the plants' tops and roots with the soil. Wait at least two weeks (four weeks if the weather has been cool) before planting the bed to give the green manure a chance to start breaking down.

HEAVY CLAY SOIL

Clay soil can be a daunting prospect when you want to start a new garden. Its tiny particles tend to pack together tightly, making it hard for tender roots to grow outward in search of water and nutrients. When dry, clays shrink into hard, dense clods that are slow to absorb moisture. When they are wet, clays hold on to water tightly and have few spaces for air. Plants suffer because the soil pores are filled with water rather than with a balance of water and air.

Fortunately, it is possible to improve clay soils. The key is to loosen the particles so that water and roots can move through the soil. Improved clays actually provide excellent growing conditions for a wide range of garden plants, since they tend to hold a good supply of both nutrients and water.

How to Identify the Problem. If your soil is high in clay, you'll notice that it's slow to warm up and dry out in spring, and you may see puddles on the soil surface hours or days after a rain. Pick up a handful of moist clay soil, and you'll notice that it feels sticky—you may even be able to mold it like modeling clay. If you try to dig or till clay soil when it is too wet, you'll find soil clinging to tools and shoes, and you'll be left with hard clumps when the soil finally dries out. And if you wait to dig until the soil is dry, you may feel you need a pickax instead of a shovel to get past the top inch or two of hard-packed soil.

Solution: Add Organic Matter. Organic matter is the answer for improving even the most forbidding clay. Digging or tilling only loosens soil temporarily, since the clay particles pack down again as they get wet. But if you mix in organic material, the particles can't join together as tightly, so they form small granules as opposed to large clods. By enlarging the spaces between particles, organic matter makes it easier for excess water to drain down through the soil. It also allows earthworms and other soil organisms to be more active, which further improves soil structure.

In this situation you may be tempted to overamend to solve clay-soil woes quickly. But in most cases you're better off spreading your soil-building efforts over several years, especially where summer droughts are common. Otherwise, the soil will be so loose and fluffy that water will drain right through before plants can get what they need.

It's also important to choose your organic matter carefully. Finely ground materials, such as peat moss, can actually make the soil stay wet longer, as they hold water and don't loosen the clay particles enough. Choose coarser materials, such as chunky compost, ground pine bark, cocoa hulls, or whatever else is available locally.

Improving Clay Soil

Organic matter is the basis for any clay-soil improvement program. Start by digging or tilling a 1-inch layer of compost, chopped leaves, or other organic matter into the planting site.

Start a clay-soil improvement program by working a 1-inch layer of organic matter into the soil in fall. (Before doing any digging or tilling, check the soil's moisture level to make sure it isn't too wet or too dry; see "Working Soil at the Right Time" on page 26 for details.) The following spring, see how the soil feels. If it is still tight and heavy, dig or till in another 1-inch layer, then plant annuals or vegetables in that spot for the summer. In fall, feel the soil again to see how it is coming along, and work in more organic matter if needed. It may take several years of this treatment to develop soil with a looser feel and more crumbly structure. Once you have achieved that, keep clay soil in good shape with regular additions of organic matter each time you prepare the bed for planting. Also keep the soil covered with organic mulch—and mulch established plantings—to protect it from compaction and to add additional organic matter.

If you aren't in a hurry to plant, growing a green manure crop and working it into the soil is a great way to loosen clay soil, add organic matter, and encourage good soil structure. For details, see "Growing Your Own Soil Amendments" on page 30.

Other Strategies. Along with regular doses of organic matter, adding gypsum (calcium sulfate) can help improve the structure of clay soil. Gypsum releases cal-

Raised beds are a good solution for a garden plagued with heavy clay soil. If you want an especially deep root run, till the site before installing and filling the beds. Raised beds provide good growing conditions for all vegetables, herbs, perennials, and other plants that thrive in well-drained conditions.

cium ions, which encourage the tiny clay particles to clump together, eventually forming crumblike aggregates. This improves air and water penetration and makes the soil more hospitable for the growth of plant roots. If you know your soil is low in calcium, apply about 4 pounds of gypsum per 100 square feet of soil; otherwise, use about 2 pounds per 100 square feet. Dig or till it into the soil when working in organic matter. Try a once-a-year application for a year or two until you notice an improvement in soil structure; then just use organic matter to help maintain the crumbly quality.

Because clay soil can be difficult to dig, you may be tempted to try improving it by adding sand. Unfortunately, adding a small percentage of sand to clay soil creates a cementlike mixture. Don't add any sand to clay unless you can add at least one-quarter by volume. That would mean working at least a 2-inch layer of sand into the top 6 inches of soil, for example—that's a lot of sand! This option is really practical only for very limited areas, such as a small flower bed or raised beds in your vegetable garden. If you choose to go this route, look for *coarse,* clean, washed sand—the washing removes salt and fine particles.

LIGHT, SANDY SOIL

Gardeners faced with clay soil may dream of having naturally loose, sandy soil. But sandy-soil gardeners have their own challenges to cope with. They're the ones dragging hoses around every summer in an effort to keep parched plantings from shriveling up altogether during dry spells. And they're the ones spending their hard-earned money on fertilizers to replace the nutrients washed out of the soil with the rapidly draining rain or irrigation water.

Identifying the Problem. If you have sandy soil, you probably know it. It's easy to feel sand's gritty texture when you rub a pinch of moist soil. It's also easy to insert a spade several inches into sandy soil. In existing garden areas, plants in sandy soil may wilt quickly without frequent watering, and they may not flower as freely or produce as well as you'd expect from their catalog description.

Solution: Add Organic Matter. The key to handling sand is the same as coping with clay: add organic matter. In this case, however, don't worry about overdoing it; add plenty, and add it often. Sandy soil holds little water to begin with, so any added organic matter will improve it. Plus, sandy soil contains lots of air, so soil organisms quickly decompose whatever you provide.

Start by adding a 2-inch layer of organic matter and working it into the soil in fall or spring. A green manure crop can also contribute significant amounts of organic matter.

If you are growing annual flowers or vegetable crops, keep adding 2 to 3 inches of organic matter a year, working it in whenever you dig or till. For perennials or ground covers, work in another 2-inch layer before planting, then mulch generously with organic matter to help maintain the humus level. Even then, organic

If you have a site with problem soil, the easiest solution is to fill it with plants that will grow in the existing conditions. Many perennials thrive in dry, sandy soil. This drought-tolerant planting features sedums, blue fescue, and mugo pine.

matter can disappear quickly. One good way to make organic matter last longer is to apply half of it as a fast-decomposing material, such as compost or grass clippings, and the rest as a longer-lasting material, such as chopped straw or ground pine bark. If perennial plantings start declining after a few years, consider lifting all the plants and digging in another 2 to 3 inches of organic matter before replanting. If that is too big a job to be practical, spot-treat special plants by digging them up every few years, mixing a shovelful of compost into the hole, and replanting.

Other Strategies. As its organic content increases, sandy soil will hold more water and dissolved nutrients, so you won't need to fertilize as often to get good growth and high yields. In the meantime, try using liquid fertilizers such as compost tea or diluted fish emulsion to give plants the nutrients they need in a form they can use quickly. (See "Making Compost Tea" on page 93.) Because the nutrients are already dissolved in water, plants can absorb them easily through their roots or leaves. Adding dry fertilizers can be wasteful, as the nutrients may wash, or leach, out of the root zone along with draining water, so your plants never get the benefit. For more information on choosing and applying liquid fertilizers, see "Granular and Liquid Fertilizers" on page 74 and "Liquid Fertilizers" on page 79.

ACID SOIL

The relative acidity or alkalinity of soil has a significant influence on how well plants grow. Even the most crumbly, rich-looking soil won't produce the best yields or the brightest flowers if the pH is much below 6. In these acid conditions, there's a good chance plants won't get the calcium, magnesium, or potassium they need, and they may get too much iron, manganese, and aluminum. Soil organisms are not as active, so organic matter is slow to break down and release nitrogen and other nutrients. These and other acid-soil problems are common in high-rainfall areas in the eastern United States and the Pacific Northwest.

Identifying the Problem. One way to judge soil acidity is to take a look at the plants that are growing well in your community, especially in natural areas. If

Plants for Acid Soil

While many plants thrive in slightly acid soil (pH 6.5 to 7.0), some tolerate or even prefer more acid conditions. The plants listed here perform well even when the pH is as low as 5.5. Not all of them will thrive in every climate, so check their descriptions in gardening reference books or ask gardening friends which ones can grow well in your area before making your final choices.

Fruits and Vegetables

Blackberries
Blueberries
Carrots
Corn
Cucumbers
Eggplant
Garlic
Onions
Parsley
Parsnips
Peppers
Potatoes (white and sweet)
Pumpkins
Raspberries
Sorrel
Strawberries
Tomatoes
Turnips
Watermelon

Flowers

Aurinia saxatilis, basket-of-gold
Aquilegia spp., columbines
Aster spp., asters
Baptisia spp., baptisias
Begonia tuberhybrida hybrids, tuberous begonias
Boltonia spp., boltonias
Chrysanthemum spp., chrysanthemums
Convallaria majalis, lily-of-the-valley
Coreopsis spp., coreopsis
Cosmos spp., cosmos
Echinacea purpurea, purple coneflower
Iberis sempervirens, perennial candytuft
Iris spp., irises (except bearded types)
Lilium spp., lilies
Liatris spp., blazing stars
Mertensia virginica, Virginia bluebells
Platycodon grandiflorus, balloon flower
Portulaca grandiflora, rock moss
Primula spp., primroses
Rudbeckia spp., black-eyed Susans
Tagetes spp., marigolds
Tropaeolum majus, nasturtium
Veronica spp., veronicas
Viola spp., pansies and violets

Trees, Shrubs, and Vines

Abies spp., firs
Calluna spp., heathers
Camellia spp., camellias
Cedrus spp., cedars
Chionanthus virginicus, fringe tree
Clethra spp., summersweets
Erica spp., heaths
Forsythia spp., forsythias
Ilex spp., hollies
Juniperus spp., junipers
Kalmia spp., mountain laurels
Lagerstroemia spp., crape myrtles
Leucothoe spp., hobblebushes
Magnolia spp., magnolias
Myrica spp., bayberries
Parthenocissus quinquefolius, Virginia creeper
Picea spp., spruces
Pieris japonica, Japanese pieris
Quercus spp., oaks
Rhododendron spp., azaleas and rhododendrons
Taxus spp., yews
Tsuga spp., hemlocks

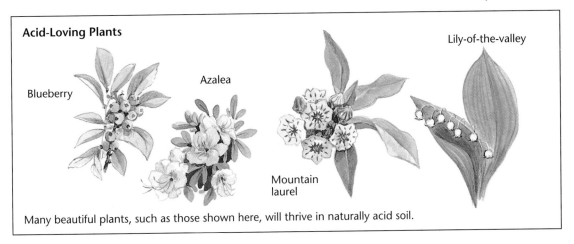

Acid-Loving Plants

Lily-of-the-valley

Azalea

Blueberry

Mountain laurel

Many beautiful plants, such as those shown here, will thrive in naturally acid soil.

acid-loving plants such as rhododendrons, mountain laurels, and blueberries are thriving there, it's likely that the soil in your area is naturally on the acid side.

To get a more accurate assessment, test the pH of a soil sample from your property, either by using a home soil-test kit or by sending it to a lab. For details on this process, refer back to "Soil pH" on page 16.

Solution: Raise the pH. Fortunately, it's fairly simple and inexpensive to raise soil pH by adding lime. Fine-ground limestone (calcium carbonate) and dolomitic limestone (which contains both magnesium carbonate and calcium carbonate) are the cheapest, easiest, safest to use, and most readily available forms of lime for the garden. The advantage of dolomitic limestone is that it supplies magnesium, an essential plant nutrient, along with releasing calcium and reducing acidity. Both forms of lime are ground-up rock. The more finely ground they are, the better, since small particles act more quickly than larger ones to neutralize soil acids. Check the label on the lime you buy to make sure that at least 50 percent will pass through a 100-mesh screen. Avoid products labeled as hydrated lime, slaked lime, builder's lime, or quicklime; these caustic powders can damage your skin as well as tender plant roots and soil organisms.

The amount of lime needed to change the pH depends on the soil's texture and the amount of organic matter it contains. The finer the texture or the greater the amount of organic matter, the more lime will be required to raise or lower the pH. That means clay soils are more resistant to change than sandy ones, for example. A general rule of thumb is that you can raise the pH of 100 square feet 1 point by adding 7 to 9 pounds of lime to a clay soil, around 5 pounds to a loam, or 2 to 3 pounds to a sandy soil. But for the most accurate results, follow the suggested amounts included with your soil-test results.

For best results, spread the lime over the area before planting, and then dig or till it in to mix it thoroughly with the soil. Lime can be applied in any season, but fall is usually the best time, giving it a chance to work before spring planting. In lawn areas and established plantings, you can apply the lime to the surface and water it in, but the results will be slower.

If you wish to raise the pH of your acid soil by more than 1 point, it's a good idea to apply small doses of lime once or twice each year over a period of several years, rather than trying to make a major change all at once. Lime has a slow and gradual effect on soil pH, but it eventually does its job. Retest the pH every year or two to monitor the changes. Once it is up to 6.5, you can wait three to four years before testing again and reliming if needed.

Other Strategies. Adding organic matter is a good way to help reduce the effects of an acid pH. Among all of its other benefits, organic matter acts as a buffer, helping to neutralize both acidity and alkalinity. Try digging or tilling in a 1- to 2-inch layer of compost, chopped leaves, or other organic matter each time you prepare soil for planting (in addition to liming).

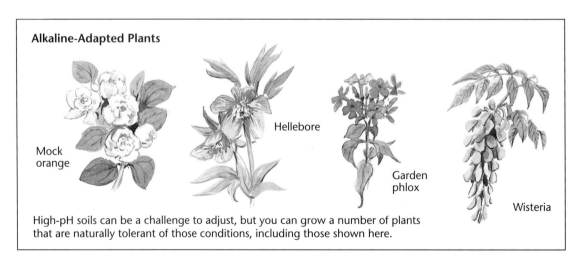

Alkaline-Adapted Plants

Mock orange

Hellebore

Garden phlox

Wisteria

High-pH soils can be a challenge to adjust, but you can grow a number of plants that are naturally tolerant of those conditions, including those shown here.

ALKALINE SOIL

A high soil pH can be as much of a problem as a low pH, and it's a bit more challenging to make a long-lasting change. Alkaline soil is common in dry parts of the western United States, but it can also occur in other areas where the soils have formed from weathered limestone. Even if the soil in your area is normally acid, soil close to your home's foundation may be on the alkaline side due to lime leaching from the cement.

Plants for Alkaline Soil

A number of plants can tolerate a pH up to 7.2 or so. If your soil's pH is higher than that, you may decide to stick with alkaline-adapted plants—at least in some parts of your garden—rather than trying to acidify your whole property. The following plants can usually tolerate a pH up to around 8. Not all will grow equally well in all climates, so research their specific needs in gardening reference books or ask gardening friends which ones they suggest before making final choices.

Vegetables	Flowers	Trees, Shrubs, and Vines
Asparagus	*Alcea rosea*, hollyhock	*Aristolochia* spp., Dutchman's pipes
Broccoli	*Canna* spp., cannas	*Catalpa* spp., catalpas
Cabbage	*Cosmos* spp., cosmos	*Gleditsia triacanthos*, honey locust
Cauliflower	*Crocus* spp., crocuses	*Gymnocladus dioicus*, Kentucky
Garlic	*Dianthus* spp., pinks	coffee tree
Leeks	*Galanthus* spp., snowdrops	*Hedera* spp., ivies
Lettuce	*Gypsophila paniculata*, baby's-breath	*Laburnum* spp., golden-chain trees
Spinach	*Helleborus* spp., hellebores	*Lonicera* spp., honeysuckles
	Hibiscus moscheutos, rose mallow	*Parthenocissus tricuspidata*, Boston ivy
	Hypericum spp., hypericums	*Philadelphus coronarius*, mock orange
	Iris bearded hybrids, bearded irises	*Platanus* spp., sycamores
	Myosotis spp., forget-me-nots	*Robinia pseudoacacia*, black locust
	Phlox spp., phloxes	*Wisteria* spp., wisterias
	Scilla spp., squills	
	Sempervivum tectorum, hen-and-chickens	
	Verbena spp., verbenas	

Identifying the Problem. One visual clue to high soil pH is plant leaves with green veins and yellow tissue in between. This is generally a symptom of iron deficiency, a condition that's common in alkaline soil. Azaleas, rhododendrons, and pin oaks (*Quercus palustris*) are commonly afflicted when grown in alkaline soil. The best way to diagnose a high pH is through a soil test, either with a home soil-test kit or through a lab.

Solution: Lower the pH. Applying sulfur is the fastest way to lower soil pH. Elemental sulfur, often called flowers of sulfur, is a yellow powder that reacts quickly with water to form sulfuric acid, which acidifies the soil. Sulfur can lower soil pH in as little as six to eight weeks, but the treatment isn't long-lasting, so you'll need to repeat it every six to twelve months.

The amount of elemental sulfur needed depends on the soil's texture and organic content. The finer the texture and the more organic matter the soil contains, the more sulfur you'll need to add. A general rule for lowering pH is to add about 1 pound of elemental sulfur per 100 square feet at a time. For best results, though, follow the recommendations that are included with your soil-test results. As with raising pH, it's best to work on lowering it gradually rather than applying a large amount of sulfur all at once. Repeat the 1-pound applications each spring and fall (testing before each application to make sure you need it) until the pH reaches the desired level.

Spread the sulfur over the area you want to treat at least a month before planting, and dig or till it in to mix it with the soil. Once plantings are established, a generous layer of organic mulch helps keep the pH lowered. Test again every three to four years to check the pH. If the results show that the pH is rising again, try pulling back the mulch each year and applying a light dusting of sulfur to the soil, then replacing the mulch.

Other Strategies. Here again, organic matter can play a vital role in lowering pH, in conjunction with adding sulfur. Peat moss, composted sawdust or bark, composted leaves, and pine needles all release carbonic acid as they decompose. Added to alkaline soil as an amendment or mulch, they have a slow, long-term effect on lowering soil pH. Other forms of organic matter, such as regular compost or grass clippings, can also help, if the other materials aren't available. The key is to raise the overall organic matter content by digging or tilling in a 1- to 2-inch layer of organic material each time you prepare the soil for planting.

One thing to keep in mind is that not all leaves help lower pH. In fact, leaves from some trees, such as green ash (*Fraxinus pennsylvanica*), can actually contribute to soil alkalinity. Oaks and maples, on the other hand, can produce slightly acidic compost, which is what you need to help lower pH. If you want to use leaf-based compost to counteract alkalinity, it's smart to test its pH first to make sure you'll get the results you're looking for.

SALINE OR SODIC SOIL

In some areas of the country, especially in the arid West and along seacoasts, gardeners have a major challenge to face: excessive salts in their soil. There are actually two different kinds of salty soil: *saline* and *sodic*. Saline soils are high in calcium and magnesium salts, and they tend to have a pH lower than 8.5. Sodic soils are high in sodium and have a pH above 8.5. Saline-sodic soils have a mix of these problems, with relatively high sodium but a lower pH.

Each situation presents its own challenges. In saline soil, the problem is mainly the high amount of salts dissolved in the soil water. To equalize the salt concentrations inside and outside plant roots, water moves out of the roots and into the soil, resulting in wilting and poor growth. Sodic soils harm plants in other ways. Besides the problems caused by their high pH, the high amount of sodium can be toxic to plants. Excess sodium also leads to poor soil structure, breaking those desirable, crumblike granules into a fine powder.

Identifying the Problem. If you live in an arid climate, there's a good chance you have salty soil. In fact, you may be able to tell you have a salt problem just by looking at your soil. Saline soil is sometimes referred to as "white alkali" because it has a light-colored salt crust. In sodic soil, humus particles are dispersed as the soil structure breaks down, and these particles may float up to the surface, creating noticeable dark patches. That's why sodic soils are also known as "black alkali."

In other cases, you may not see any obvious signs of salt, but your plants grow poorly and produce disappointing yields. If you suspect a problem, have your soil checked by a soil-testing lab to check the balance of nutrients. For more details, see "Testing Your Soil's Fertility" on page 15.

Solution: Treat the Soil. This is one situation where organic matter alone can't achieve the results you need. Adding organic matter will help to some extent, especially in saline conditions, by counteracting the sodium's tendency to break down soil aggregates (those desirable crumbly granules). Organic matter also helps keep sodic soil structurally sound. And in either situation, it's smart to cover the soil with an organic mulch. This reduces the amount of water that evaporates from the soil's surface, so water is less likely to be drawn upward, carrying those salts into the root zone.

The real key, though, is either to reduce the amount of salts or to convert them to compounds that are less harmful to plants. Drenching saline soil with large amounts of water helps leach the salts down deeper into the soil and away from the root zone. For this to work, of course, the irrigation water must be low in salt and your soil must drain freely. Otherwise, the water just carries more salt into the root zone.

If you have sodic soil, it's best to first apply gypsum (calcium sulfate) to the soil surface at a rate of about 10 pounds per 100 square feet of garden area. Then keep the area moist. This helps convert at least some of the toxic materials into less harmful compounds. After a week or two, leach the soil by drenching it several times with water to help wash out the salts.

Other Strategies. Another option is to stick with plants that are naturally adapted to your particular conditions. Because those conditions can vary widely, depending on your site, climate, and soil, it's hard to generalize about which plants will thrive there. One way to get ideas is to visit local natural areas and walk around your neighborhood to see what is growing well. You can get excellent pointers on dealing with salty soil by talking to local gardeners.

COMPACTED SOIL

Garden soil should have plenty of pores between the particles of mineral and organic matter. Some soils, however, may be so compacted that these pores are

Installing steppingstones in your garden helps reduce soil compaction. They're handy for maintenance in perennial gardens and great where foot traffic has resulted in worn, compacted areas through flower or shrub beds or in the lawn.

closed off. This compaction may be the result of natural forces or of human activity; in either case, it has undesirable consequences. If the soil is compacted near the surface, rainfall or irrigation water runs off instead of soaking in. If drainage is blocked by a subsurface compacted layer, the surface soil is likely to become waterlogged. Tough-rooted trees and shrubs can usually penetrate these tight layers, but many annual and perennial plants cannot.

Identifying the Problem. Soil compaction is a common problem around newly built homes, where construction equipment, trucks, and foot traffic have packed down the soil enough to damage it. You may not notice the problem until you try to dig, when you find that the soil is rock-hard. Worn areas and bare spots in the lawn or ground cover plantings are also common signs of surface compaction due to foot traffic.

If there is a compacted zone below the surface, you may notice that the soil stays soggy for long periods (several days or more) after heavy rains. Try digging a hole at least 1 foot deep in the affected area to see if you run into a tight, hard-to-dig layer—a sign of compaction.

Solution: Loosen the Soil. For smaller areas (such as individual flower beds), hand-digging and tilling are good ways to loosen compacted soil. The fastest way to treat large areas is to hire tractor-drawn equipment that can break through the compacted zone. This leaves the surface rough, and you'll have to spend some time with a tiller or hand tools to smooth the area for planting.

An alternative, if you have more time and patience, is to plant a green manure crop of a deep-rooted legume, such as sweet clover or alfalfa. After a year or two of vigorous growth, the roots of these plants will have penetrated several feet down in the soil. Then mow down the crop and dig or till both the roots and the tops into the soil before planting a lawn or making beds or borders.

When you are treating any compacted area, you should add plenty of organic matter to improve soil structure and help it stay loose and porous for a period of months or even years. Each time you dig or till, work a 1- to 2-inch layer of compost or other organic matter into the soil.

Preventing Further Compaction. It is easier to prevent soil compaction than it is to "cure" it. If you are planning new construction or home renovations, discuss your concerns with the contractor. Use fences or other barricades to restrict vehicle movement to driveways and designated parking spots whenever possible.

Clearly marked walkways help direct foot traffic around your home and through your garden, preventing the formation of compacted trails through lawn areas or planted beds. But before installing new paths and walkways, take a look at existing worn areas to see where family and visitors naturally tend to walk. There's usually a good reason those paths are there! Rather than trying to redirect foot traffic, consider incorporating those informal paths into your walkway plans. The solution could be as simple as adding steppingstones across lawns and beds or as formal as an elegant brick path.

Keep in mind that tilling planting areas repeatedly to the same depth can create a compacted zone just below that depth, so vary the setting on your tiller and try hand-digging every few years to loosen that lower layer. To retain the benefits of your soil-building efforts, avoid walking on the soil in prepared beds. If you can't reach all parts of a bed from the perimeter for planting and maintenance, add a few steppingstones for permanent footing or lay a few broad boards on the soil to step on, then remove them after planting. A thin layer of mulch helps protect exposed soil from compaction by heavy rain until plantings fill in.

WET SOIL

Soggy spots in the lawn and garden can be a real gardening challenge. Water tends to accumulate in low spots, flat places, and areas where the soil is compacted, shallow, or underlain by an impermeable layer. If you walk or work in that area, wet spots can quickly turn into messy mud puddles. And many common garden plants will die if their roots are under water for an extended period of time.

Sometimes it is easy to solve the problem by loosening the soil or building raised planting beds; other situations may call for professional advice and regrading or drainage installation. But if you don't have to walk through that area, consider creating a beautiful garden feature by planting a variety of moisture-loving flowers, shrubs, and trees.

Identifying the Problem. It's easy to identify wet spots: look for areas of standing water or places where the soil "squishes" when you walk. Depending on the source of the water, the spots may be dry in some seasons and wet in others. Plants in these areas may grow poorly or die because of root rot.

Wet spots can be caused by surface water that doesn't drain down or by water coming up from below the surface. When you dig a hole, you may notice that the subsurface soil has a grayish cast (due to constant submersion in water) or a mix of orangish and grayish areas (indicating alternate waterlogging and dryness).

Solution: Dig Deeply. If you find a dense, hard-to-dig layer within the top foot or so of soil, you may be able to solve the problem by digging or tilling deeply to break up that impermeable layer. For more information, see "Solution: Loosen the Soil" on page 46.

Solution: Install Drainage. In some cases the problem may be that excess water is running off one area of your property and collecting in another spot faster than

Plants for Wet Places

If your yard has a troublesome wet spot, you might choose to "go with the flow" and plant accordingly. Although many plants can't tolerate continually damp conditions, some beautiful ones grow very well with "wet feet." Some moisture-loving flowers, shrubs, and trees are listed below. Keep in mind that not all of these plants will thrive in all climates, so check a gardening reference book or ask at a local nursery before making your choices.

Flowers

Astilbe spp., astilbes
Caltha palustris, marsh marigold
Eupatorium purpureum, Joe-Pye weed
Hibiscus moscheutos, rose mallow
Iris pseudacorus, yellow flag iris
Ligularia spp., ligularias
Lobelia cardinalis, cardinal flower
Lysimachia nummularia, creeping Jenny
Matteuccia struthiopteris, ostrich fern
Mimulus guttatus, money flower
Onoclea sensibilis, sensitive fern
Osmunda regalis, royal fern
Primula japonica, Japanese primrose
Rodgersia spp., rodgersias

Shrubs and Trees

Acer rubrum, red maple
Aronia arbutifolia, red chokeberry
Betula nigra, river birch
Carex spp., sedges
Clethra alnifolia, summersweet
Cornus alba and *C. sericea*, red-twigged dogwoods
Ilex verticillata, winterberry
Metasequoia glyptostroboides, dawn redwood
Nyssa sylvatica, sour gum
Platanus spp., sycamores
Populus deltoides, cottonwood
Rhododendron viscosum, swamp azalea
Salix spp., willows

it can soak in. Redirecting the runoff water can help keep prime gardening areas dry while channeling it to a place (another garden bed, for example) where you can use it or to a site where it can drain undisturbed. This may involve digging a few shallow drainage ditches (and planting them with grass or a low-growing ground cover) to intercept and divert water flowing down a slope. Or it may call for more involved work, such as major regrading or installing subsurface drainage. If you are having serious problems with wet spots, standing water, or water running into your home, consult a professional landscape architect.

Solution: Build Raised Beds. Sometimes neither deep-digging nor installed drainage is possible or practical. Fortunately, you have another option: building raised beds several inches above the existing soil surface. In a raised bed excess surface water drains away more quickly, and the rooting zone is lifted above sub-surface waterlogging. Those extra few inches of well-drained soil can mean the difference between healthy, vigorous growth and death—especially during cool, wet weather, when the soil tends to stay saturated longer.

Depending on the severity of the drainage problem, you can raise beds anywhere from 3 to 12 inches or more. Just remember that the higher the bed, the faster it will dry out. In most areas, a bed 4 to 6 inches high provides the right balance of drainage and moisture. A bed this depth won't require a frame to keep the soil in place, but you may choose to enclose it anyway, for good looks and easy maintenance. In the vegetable garden, good options include cement blocks (also known as cinder blocks) or 2 by 6 planks set on their narrow side and held in place by short stakes. In flower beds, low stone or brick walls are an attractive option. Inside the frame, prepare the bed as the soil and your plants require, adding organic matter such as compost and additional soil brought in from elsewhere to fill it.

Raised Beds for Wet Spots

Raising the soil level gives your plants more well-drained rooting room, so you can grow a wide range of plants in what once was a soggy spot. Framing the sides of the bed with cinder blocks or boards is fine for vegetables; rocks make a more attractive setting for flowers and herbs.

When planting shrubs and trees in wet areas, you can get similar benefits by shallow planting. Instead of digging a hole, simply loosen the surface soil, set the root ball on top, and mound more soil over and around the roots. This protects the plant's crown—the junction between roots and stems—from excess moisture and guarantees that the fine roots near the surface will be in well-drained soil. Deeper roots can reach down for water in the underlying soil.

SLOPING SITES

Gentle slopes can be a great garden feature, adding visual interest and providing a variety of moist and well-drained planting areas. But if you are trying to cope with steep slopes, you may wish your property were as flat as a board. Slopes can be a real hassle, and even a danger, to mow. But if you don't keep some kind of plants growing there, you're stuck looking at worn, eroded earth where rains have carved out deep channels. Establishing plants on a slope can be difficult, though, as water runs off quickly, leaving the soil parched after all but the heaviest rain.

Identifying the Problem. If you have troublesome slopes, you know it. You are probably the one who has to maintain them, either by mowing or by cleaning up the soil and debris that washes down them.

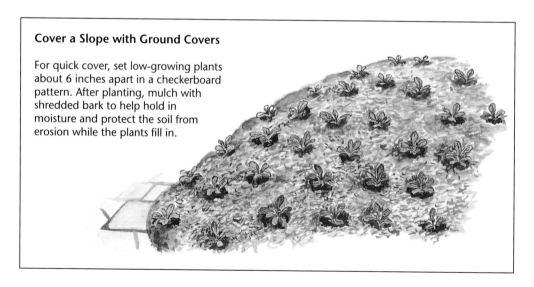

Cover a Slope with Ground Covers

For quick cover, set low-growing plants about 6 inches apart in a checkerboard pattern. After planting, mulch with shredded bark to help hold in moisture and protect the soil from erosion while the plants fill in.

Ground Covers for Slopes

Ground covers are fast-growing plants that tend to creep or sprawl along the ground, quickly filling in to create a carpet of leaves and stems. Ground covers for slopes have to be especially tough to tolerate the often-dry conditions. Here's a listing of a few excellent choices for these difficult sites. Keep in mind that not all of these plants will thrive in the same climates and light conditions, so check with a gardening reference book or with local gardening friends before finalizing your choices.

Achillea tomentosa, woolly yarrow
Ajuga reptans, ajuga
Euonymus fortunei, winter creeper
Hedera helix, English ivy
Hemerocallis fulva, tawny daylily
Hypericum calycinum, Saint-John's-wort
Juniperus horizontalis, creeping juniper

Oenothera speciosa, showy sundrops
Pachysandra terminalis, Japanese pachysandra
Phlox subulata, moss phlox
Potentilla fruticosa, shrubby cinquefoil
Rosa rugosa, rugosa rose
Vinca spp., periwinkles

Solution: Plant Ground Covers. One attractive, low-maintenance option is to cover the slope with tough ground covers. You won't have to mow them, and they'll provide a good-looking carpet of foliage to shield your soil from erosion. Some even offer colorful flowers, turning a problem site into a beautiful garden feature. See "Ground Covers for Slopes" above for suggestions.

The closer you set the plants at first, the faster your planting will fill in. In all but the smallest sites, though, buying enough ground covers to plant closely can be quite expensive. A good compromise is to set the plants about 6 inches apart (12 to 18 inches apart for larger plants, such as junipers and roses). To determine how many plants you need, multiply the width of the bed by its length (both in inches) and divide by 6 (or 12 to 18 for larger plants). Before buying all the plants, consider checking with gardening friends to see if they have any extras: most people have ground covers in excess once they get them going.

Start planting at the top of the slope and work down. Stagger the placement of the plants in a checkerboard pattern to evenly cover the area. Mulch the bare soil between them with a moderately coarse mulch, such as shredded bark, which will be less likely to be washed away by heavy rain than a lightweight mulch. Be prepared to water every week or two for the first growing season to ensure that the plants get established.

Soil Mixes for Container Plants

Plants growing in containers require fertile, well-drained soil, just as those growing in the ground do, but garden soil is seldom a good choice for filling pots, planters, and window boxes. Besides making containers very heavy, garden soil tends to pack down, interfering with proper drainage and smothering the roots. A commercial or homemade mix will give you much better results.

A good-quality planting medium needs a mixture of coarse and fine particles to hold moisture while allowing excess water to drain away. It should contain a generous supply of nutrients, since the area the roots can explore is limited by the size of the container.

You can fill containers with either a commercially prepared medium or your own mix. Commercial "potting soil" usually is a blend of peat moss and vermiculite (for water retention) and perlite (for drainage), sometimes with a synthetic fertilizer (avoid these if your garden is strictly organic). Composted bark is another common ingredient. These mixes are convenient to handle, and you can use them straight out of the bag if you are growing annuals or vegetables in the containers. If the plants will stay in the containers for more than one growing season, it's worth adding some compost or good garden soil to the mix. These materials will help hold moisture while providing a small but steady supply of nutrients. Add one part compost and/or soil for every six parts of commercial potting mix.

If you have a number of containers to fill, or if you want an all-organic potting soil, you may want to mix your own growing medium. There are as many recipes for potting soil as there are gardeners who make it, but here's one to get you started:

4 parts peat moss

1 part perlite (a heat-treated volcanic material available at garden centers)

1 part compost or leaf mold (or half compost and half good garden soil)

$1/2$ ounce of limestone per gallon of peat moss

Put all of the materials into a large tub or a wheelbarrow and mix thoroughly with a shovel. Wear a mask—this can be a dusty job! Before filling your containers, add water to the mix to moisten it. You want it to be damp to the touch but not so wet that water oozes out when you lightly squeeze a handful.

If you're growing plants that appreciate extra-rich soil, add more compost. For a drier, faster-draining mix, add more perlite or composted pine or fir bark chips. You can add a balanced organic fertilizer (according to suggested rates on the label) for more nutrients. A small amount of garden soil is also a good nutrient source, but don't be tempted to use large amounts or to use it by itself.

Terraces can transform a sloping site, where erosion can be a big problem, into a series of level garden beds that are easy to care for. This gentle slope, terraced with railroad ties, is planted with perennials, herbs, and annuals.

Solution: Build Terraces. Another way to slow the flow of water is to reshape the slope into a series of stepped beds, commonly called terraces. Terracing can be as simple as building a low wall of soil on the downhill side of each new groundcover plant. A slightly more formal approach is to create the walls on the downhill side out of rocks, bricks, or wood. Then fill in behind the walls with a mix of topsoil and organic matter to create flat-surfaced planting areas. In large areas, terracing can be a big job. Not only will you need to construct sturdy walls to hold the soil, you'll also need to move a lot of soil around to level the beds. But in exchange for that one-time effort, you can enjoy the extra planting space for years to come.

Other Strategies. Water tends to run off the surface of a sloping garden unless the soil is very permeable so that water soaks in very rapidly. Improving soil structure and loosening compacted areas will help increase water penetration. If you don't choose to plant ground covers, at least shield the soil with a generous layer of mulch year-round.

CHAPTER 3
MULCHES

While working organic matter into your soil is a key step in creating a great garden, spreading a layer of organic matter as mulch over your soil also provides a wide range of benefits. A well-chosen mulch keeps your soil, plants, and garden in top condition in a variety of ways.

- **Suppresses Weeds.** Mulch blocks light from reaching the soil, so many weed seeds don't get the light they need to sprout. And any weeds that do emerge are easier to pull, as the soil below the mulch stays moist and loose.
- **Conserves Moisture.** Mulch shields the soil from sun and wind, greatly reducing water loss through evaporation, so you don't have to water as often.
- **Increases Soil Organic Matter.** Organic mulches such as chopped leaves and compost also add a small but steady amount of organic matter and nutrients to the soil, even though you don't dig them in. Organisms in the soil decompose them, and soil dwellers such as earthworms help move the organic matter down into lower soil layers.

Bark mulch gives a neat, finished look to garden beds while protecting the soil. The larger the bark pieces, the longer the mulch will last. To add nutrients and a ready source of organic matter to the soil, pull back the mulch in spring, add a layer of compost, then replace the bark.

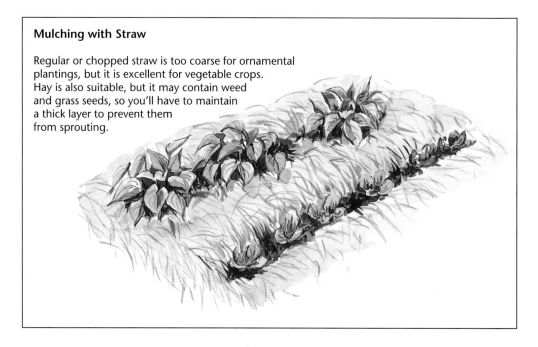

Mulching with Straw

Regular or chopped straw is too coarse for ornamental plantings, but it is excellent for vegetable crops. Hay is also suitable, but it may contain weed and grass seeds, so you'll have to maintain a thick layer to prevent them from sprouting.

- **Prevents Erosion and Compaction.** Soil protected by mulch is less prone to damage from heavy rain, so it keeps its desirable crumbly structure. Soil with good structure is less likely to erode, since water percolates down through it rather than running off it.
- **Keeps Leaves and Flowers Clean.** Mulch prevents soil from splashing up on plants and produce, so flowers stay mud-free and vegetable and herb harvests are easier to clean. Soil splashing onto plants can carry disease-causing organisms, and mulch helps minimize this problem.
- **Moderates Soil Temperature.** In summer, mulch keeps the soil from getting too hot, so earthworms and other beneficial soil organisms stay comfortable. And in winter, mulch minimizes rapid thawing and refreezing during mild days and cold nights, preventing damage to perennial plants.

To get the most benefit for your garden, it pays to choose the right mulch and manage it properly through the seasons. In exchange, you'll reap the rewards of a healthy, productive, easy-care garden all year long.

CHOOSING THE RIGHT MULCH

With so many materials to choose from, choosing the right mulch may seem confusing. Fortunately, most mulches work equally well in a variety of situations. To get the most for your money—and for the time you spend spreading the material—it's worth considering several factors, including what the mulch is made from, how it looks, how long it lasts, and how much it costs.

Inorganic versus Organic. One characteristic to keep in mind is whether the mulch is organic (derived from previously living material) or inorganic. Inorganic mulches include materials such as crushed stone, gravel, and plastic. Stone-based mulches are uniform and long-lasting, making them ideal for pathways. Black

In the vegetable garden, mulching with black plastic has some advantages, although it doesn't do anything to improve the soil. Use it to prewarm the soil for heat-loving crops such as eggplants and melons.

Crushed stone or gravel is a handsome, long-lasting mulch for permanent plantings such as this specimen grouping of evergreens. It is also commonly used to mulch rock gardens and pathways.

Common Mulch Materials

Material	Advantages	Disadvantages	Thickness	Comments
Bark (chipped, ground, or shredded)	Attractive and easy to apply.	Some bark may be acidic. Expensive for large areas. Harbors some insects.	2 to 3 in.	Size of pieces varies. The larger the pieces, the longer the mulch will last.
Compost	Excellent organic mulch. Adds nutrients and organic matter to soil. Attractive, natural appearance.	May harbor weed seeds.	1 to 2 in.	Dark, crumbly "finished" compost breaks down quickly, so top it with a coarser, longer-lasting material in perennial, shrub, and tree plantings.
Corncobs (ground)	Easy to apply. Natural appearance.	Takes nitrogen from the soil as it decomposes.	3 to 4 in.	Apply over a layer of compost or grass clippings, or add blood meal to provide extra nitrogen.
Grass clippings	Easily available. Decomposes quickly to add organic matter and nutrients to soil.	Sometimes contains weed seeds. Thick layers can mat down and smother plants. May be contaminated by chemical sprays.	$1/2$ to 1 in.	Apply a thin layer several times through the season. Or top with a layer of coarser, longer-lasting material. Do not use clippings from sprayed lawns.
Hay and straw	Easy to apply. Readily available in most areas. Natural appearance.	May contain seeds. Susceptible to fire and wind.	6 to 8 in.	Ideal for mulching vegetable gardens and fruit plantings. Straw is less likely to contain unwanted seeds.
Leaf mold (composted leaves)	A great organic mulch. Natural appearance. Adds nutrients and organic matter to soil.	Requires time and a large quantity of leaves to make. May be too lumpy for high-visibility areas.	3 to 4 in.	To make your supply go farther, top a 2-inch layer with an attractive, longer-lasting mulch, such as shredded bark.
Leaves	Natural appearance. Adds nutrients and organic matter to soil.	Whole leaves may mat down and smother delicate plants.	3 to 4 in.	Chop leaves with a shredder or bagging mower before applying.
Newspaper	Readily available. Decomposes quickly.	Unattractive but can be covered with a more decorative mulch.	$1/4$ in.	Use under bark chips for vegetable garden paths or for mulching new shrub plantings.
Peat moss	Natural appearance.	Expensive. Crusts over when dry; hard to rewet.		Not recommended for use as a mulch.
Pine needles	Readily available. Natural appearance. Adds organic matter to soil.	Tends to make soil slightly acid.	2 to 3 in.	Great for mulching acid-loving plants, such as azaleas and blueberries. For other plants, add a sprinkling of lime to balance the pH.

"Homegrown" Mulches

If you have deciduous trees on your property, chances are you have an ample supply of leaves each fall. Whole leaves can pack down and smother plants, but if they are chopped—either in a shredder or by a lawn mower with a bag attached—they create a uniform, attractive mulch that's ideal for any part of the garden.

plastic mulch is often used in the vegetable garden to help warm the soil for heat-loving crops such as melons; it usually lasts only a year or so.

While both inorganic and organic mulches will cover the soil, only organic materials will improve it. Organic mulches come in a wide price range, so you can choose those that are best suited for your budget. In fact, homemade materials, such as compost and chopped leaves, make excellent mulches for free—a price that's hard to beat. Commercially produced mulches, on the other hand, offer convenience for a price and are available by the bag or the truckload.

Appearance. The best mulch for a garden depends on where you plan to use it. In high-visibility areas, such as those close to the house, it's best to stick with good-looking, medium-textured, uniform mulches such as shredded bark or bark chips. In annual beds, you can get away with less uniform but finer-textured materials, such as compost, chopped leaves, leaf mold (composted leaves), or grass clippings, because the plants will quickly hide the mulch. Plus it will be easy to dig or till in whatever mulch remains at the end of the season to improve the soil. Coarse materials, such as ground corncobs, hay, and straw, are relatively inexpensive and make excellent, lightweight mulches, but they aren't attractive enough for decorative plantings, so save them for your vegetable and fruit plantings.

Permanence. In general, the coarser the material, the longer it will last. Fine materials, such as grass clippings or screened compost, can break down within a

Mulching with Pine Needles

Needles from evergreen trees tend to acidify the soil as they break down, so they are ideal for mulching acid-loving plants such as azaleas and rhododendrons.

few months, so you'll need to reapply them every few months to keep them at the ideal thickness. Very coarse mulches, such as bark chunks, can last for several years. The faster a mulch breaks down, however, the more quickly it adds organic matter to your soil.

Availability. Unless you're lucky enough to have an unlimited gardening budget, you'll need to consider how much each mulch will cost. As mentioned above, recycled materials such as compost, chopped leaves, and grass clippings are free for the making (or collecting). If you don't have enough compost, see if your community makes and supplies it to local residents. And nongardening neighbors may be more than willing to let you rake and collect their leaves to supplement your own supply.

Mulches for Containers

When you're spreading mulch on your garden, don't forget to save some for your container plantings! A mulch will help keep the growing medium from drying out so quickly, so you won't have to water your pots and planters as often. Organic mulches, such as compost and leaf mold, will add some nutrients through the season as they break down. Mulch also gives a container a nice "finished" look before the plants fill in to cover the growing medium. For annual containers, choose a mulch that will break down by the end of the season: compost, leaf mold, and cocoa bean hulls are good choices. Keep more permanent mulches, such as gravel or shredded bark, for long-term plantings, such as potted perennials and shrubs. Whichever material you choose, apply a $1/2$ to 1-inch layer right after planting and watering the container.

When building a new garden bed, keep the soil mulched from the outset with whatever material is handy. Mulch discourages weed seeds from germinating and protects the newly turned soil. A thick layer of newspaper under the mulch is further protection against weeds.

Depending on where you live, you may have access to some processing by-products, such as cocoa bean hulls. (Gardening friends are an excellent source of advice on finding and using locally available materials.) These materials can make great mulches and are often much cheaper than material trucked in from other areas. You may have to go pick them up yourself, however. If convenience is important, you may prefer to spend a little more to buy bagged mulches or have a truckload delivered.

APPLYING MULCHES

Mulching is one of the most satisfying and rewarding garden chores. Although it takes time and effort, your plantings will look great after they are mulched, and you will have saved yourself a lot of weeding, watering, and other work later on.

When to Mulch. New plantings benefit from mulching right away, whatever the season. The mulch will help keep the soil moist and at a moderate temperature, encouraging the plants to send out new roots.

After the first year, plan on mulching your plantings at least once a year. Many gardeners prefer to mulch in late spring, when the soil has had a chance to warm up and dry out a bit from spring rains. It is important that the soil be moist

**Mulches for
Low-Maintenance Areas**

Coarse, woody mulches, such as
bark chunks, can take several years
to break down, so they are a good
choice for tree and shrub
plantings.

when you mulch, however; otherwise the mulch may soak up rain or irrigation
water before it can soak through to the soil. (If the top 2 or 3 inches of soil are
dry, it's smart to water before mulching.) And don't expect mulch to smother
existing weeds; weed thoroughly before applying any mulch.

How Much Mulch? The thickness of the layer depends on the mulch you are
using. In general, the looser the mulch, the thicker it can be. You need enough
material to keep the soil covered, but not so much that it will smother the

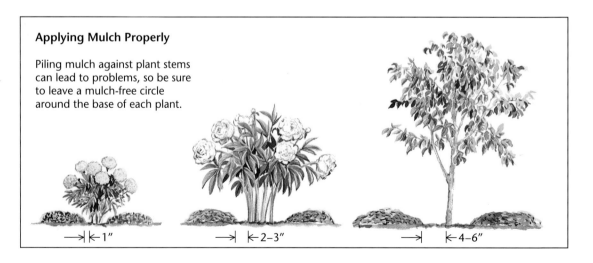

Applying Mulch Properly

Piling mulch against plant stems
can lead to problems, so be sure
to leave a mulch-free circle
around the base of each plant.

1"   2–3"   4–6"

plants. For the recommended depths of many popular mulches, see "Common Mulch Materials" on page 58. While even a thin layer of mulch will help, it's best not to skimp when applying it, especially if you want to suppress weeds.

When spreading mulch, avoid piling it around or over the base of your plants. Mulch piled in this manner holds extra moisture around the stems, encouraging rot. It also provides a great hiding place for voles and other pests that munch on plants. To prevent these problems, leave a mulch-free zone around each plant: about 1 inch from annual stems, 2 to 3 inches from perennial stems, and 4 to 6 inches from shrub stems and tree trunks.

MANAGING MULCHES

A little care through the year will help keep your mulches—and your garden—in top shape. You may need to add more mulch to keep it at the right thickness, or you may be able to just fluff up what's there.

Maintaining Mulch Layers. Organic mulches will decompose over time, so eventually you'll need to add more to keep them at the desired depth. Bark chunks can last for four years or more, while shredded bark may stay in good shape for a year or two. Compost, grass clippings, and other fine-textured mulches can break down within a few months, so you may need to reapply them twice a year—in spring and in midsummer. While these fast-decomposing materials will do great things for your soil, you may not have the time, resources, or inclination to apply mulch several times a year. To get the advantages of both coarse and fine mulches, try this trick: spread a layer of fine-textured material first (at about half the recommended thickness), then top it with a 1/2- to 1-inch layer of a coarser, longer-lasting mulch. This way you'll have to

---

TIPS FOR SUCCESS

MULCH COMBINATIONS

Combining mulches makes sense for a variety of reasons. Topping an inexpensive or free mulch with a more expensive one —grass clippings under shredded bark, for example—makes sense because it stretches your budget. This approach also makes good use of grass clippings, which might otherwise end up in a landfill.

In a new garden bed—or one where weeds have been a problem in past seasons—a thick layer of newspaper under a heavier mulch (to hold the newspaper in place) prevents weeds from reaching the surface. Spread the newspaper eight to ten sheets thick and overlap the edges (do this on a windless day!). After you've spread several sections, weight down the newspaper with handfuls of the "topping" mulch. Once you've blanketed the entire area with newspaper, cover it with the other mulch. In vegetable gardens, grass clippings work fine for a topping mulch; hay and straw are generally too light, and newspaper will blow in a high wind, at least until it has been in place for a few weeks. In areas where appearance is important, top newspaper with chipped or shredded bark.

Making the Most of Your Compost

If you don't have enough compost to use it alone as a mulch, spread a thin layer over the soil, then top it with a longer-lasting mulch, such as shredded bark.

Removing Mulches in Fall

Raking the mulch off your perennial garden in fall may keep mice and other animal pests away from your plants. You can replace the mulch once the ground freezes.

mulch only once a year. When it's time to mulch again, rake off the leftover coarse mulch, apply another layer of fine material, and rake the old mulch back over it.

Mulching through the Year. For many gardeners, a once-a-year mulching spree serves the purpose. But to get the most from your effort, a little extra attention in certain seasons is definitely worthwhile. Here is a seasonal rundown.

- In late winter, rake the mulch off your perennial plantings and pile it to the side. This will give the soil a chance to warm up and dry out.
- In early to mid-spring, dig or till the remaining mulch into annual flower and vegetable beds before planting.
- In late spring, replace mulch around perennials. In annual and vegetable gardens, mulch right after setting out transplants, or wait until emerging seedlings are 3 to 4 inches tall. This is also a good time to fluff up mulches around shrubs and trees with a pitchfork; add more mulch if necessary.
- In midsummer, check the depth of fine-textured mulches and add more material if needed to keep them at the ideal depth.

- In early fall, rake mulches away from shrubs, trees, and perennials, and pile the extra to the side. This will discourage voles, mice, and other animal pests from making their winter homes next to your plants.
- Once the soil has frozen in late fall or early winter, replace mulches around permanent plantings. By this time the pesky critters will have found other homes, and they'll be less likely to feed on the roots and stems of your plants.

Troubleshooting Mulch Problems

Mulch offers many more advantages than disadvantages, but problems can occasionally occur. Here are some common problems you may encounter and suggested solutions.

Problem	Solution
Slugs and snails seriously damage mulched plants, chewing large holes in leaves.	Mulches can provide ideal moist hiding places for these pests. Rake off the mulch to let the soil and mulch dry out, then gradually replace the mulch. If problems continue, use just a thin layer of mulch ($1/4$ to $1/2$ inch). If you still have problems, you may need to avoid mulching altogether.
Many weeds sprout through the mulch.	Weed thoroughly before applying or renewing mulch. The mulch itself may contain weed seeds and roots, so avoid adding to your compost pile weeds with creeping roots or those that have gone to seed. Topping compost with another mulch may prevent problems. Add mulch if needed to keep it at the recommended depth.
Mulched plants are slow to sprout in spring.	Heavy mulch can slow soil warming in spring. Rake mulches off perennial gardens (and shrub plantings, if necessary) in late winter to let the sun reach the soil; replace the mulch in late spring.
Mulched plants rot at the base.	Mulch can hold in too much moisture, especially if your soil is naturally wet or if the weather is cool and rainy. In these cases, apply and maintain mulch at only half the recommended depth and rake it off during very wet weather. Keep mulch several inches away from the base of plant stems.
Mulched plants grow poorly and may show yellow leaves.	Some mulches, especially "woody" materials such as fine bark chips and ground corncobs, "tie up" soil nitrogen as they break down. The nitrogen is released back into the soil later, but in the meantime your plants may lack the nitrogen they need for healthy growth. Spread a layer of compost or grass clippings under the woody mulch or add blood meal (according to package directions) to supply extra nitrogen.

Chapter 4

Fertilizers

Plants draw everything they need to live and grow from air, water, and soil. Air and water supply the carbon dioxide, hydrogen, and oxygen they need, while soil supplies all the other nutrients. The best way to ensure nutrient-rich soil is simply to follow the old organic gardener's adage—feed the soil and let the soil feed the plants.

In most cases you don't need to do anything more than feed the soil with compost and other organic matter to provide plants with the nutrients they need. In fact, many gardeners don't use fertilizer at all if their soil is well amended, but fertilizing is another obvious option for providing nutrients. Using fertilizer is a good alternative if you have a new garden where the soil is not yet up to par, or if plants show signs of nutrient deficiencies. In general, vegetable gardens, especially an intensive garden, which uses up available nutrients quickly, will need more fertilizers than flower gardens.

Before choosing a fertilizer, though, you need to know what is in your soil to start with. Plants may look nutrient-starved for a variety of reasons, and fertilizer won't fix all of the problems. For example, a soil may contain all the necessary

---

Fertilizing, monitoring pH, and building organic matter are more important in the vegetable garden than anywhere else. Fertile, friable soil is essential for most vegetable crops to produce maximum yields.

nutrients, but if they are not in the right chemical form, plants will not be able to absorb them. This is the problem if the soil is either too acid or too alkaline, for example. Some soils are naturally low in fertility; sandy soils, for instance, are not able to hold adequate nutrients for lush growth. In other cases, the natural nutrient supply has been depleted by leaching or erosion. As plants grow, they deplete soil nutrients. In nature, some of these nutrients return to the soil when leaves, branches, and stems decompose. In the garden, regular applications of compost and other organic matter can accomplish the same thing. But these processes are relatively slow, and they may not be able to keep up with your plants' needs.

Fertilizer provides nutrients that are unavailable in your soil and replaces those that your plants have used. With fertilizer, you can speed the growth and increase the size of young plants, and you can maintain the quality and healthy growth of older ones. However, incorrectly applied fertilizers can actually damage plants; to get the best possible results, it's worth taking a few minutes to learn about choosing and applying fertilizers properly.

DO YOU NEED TO FERTILIZE?

Before spending money on fertilizer or taking the time to spread it, make sure your garden needs it. Too much fertilizer is often worse than none at all. Sometimes its possible to tell which nutrients are lacking in your soil by looking at your plants. Some deficiencies have very distinctive symptoms; others just appear as overall poor growth. For an overview of the most common deficiencies and their symptoms, refer to "Identifying and Correcting Common Nutrient Deficiencies" on page 70.

For best results, though, try to correct nutrient imbalances *before* plants start showing symptoms. The most accurate way to check your garden's fertility is to test a soil sample, either with a home test kit or through a lab. (For details, see "Testing Your Soil's Fertility" on page 15.) The results will help you make an educated decision about what and how much fertilizer you need to add for the plants you want to grow. Symptoms of soil problems can mimic those of nutrient deficiencies—plants growing in compacted soil or in conditions that are too wet or too dry will exhibit overall poor growth, for example. A soil test will help you determine the true cause of the problem.

Identifying Iron Deficiency

If you notice leaves that are mostly yellow, with green only along the leaf veins, suspect an iron deficiency. In alkaline soil, iron is not readily available to plants, and by adjusting the pH to neutral or below you may be able to correct this deficiency.

Spotting a Phosphorus Deficiency

A purplish cast on leaves and stems can be a sign that a plant isn't getting enough phosphorus. Such a deficiency is especially common in seedlings because their limited root systems may not reach phosphorus reserves lower in the soil. The problem may correct itself as the weather warms up and root systems expand. In the meantime, spraying a liquid fertilizer on the leaves can help keep plants vigorous.

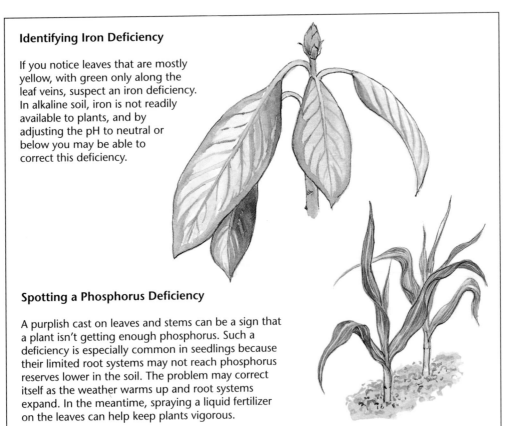

CHOOSING THE RIGHT FERTILIZER

A visit to your local garden center will demonstrate how many different fertilizer materials there are to choose from. They differ in the nutrients they contain, the origins of those nutrients, and the form of the material itself. Understanding the basic types of fertilizers will help you choose the right materials for your particular needs.

Nutrient Content. A *complete* fertilizer contains nitrogen, phosphorus, and potassium. The percentages of these elements that are immediately available to plants are represented by the series of numbers printed on the front of the fertilizer package, called the fertilizer analysis or NPK ratio. Nitrogen is listed first, fol-

Finding the Fertilizer Analysis

On any bag of fertilizer, you should see a series of three numbers. This nutrient analysis or NPK ratio indicates the relative proportions of nitrogen, phosphate (phosphorus), and potash (potassium) in the product. A complete fertilizer has all three components, a simple fertilizer contains one, and a compound fertilizer contains two of these essential nutrients.

Identifying and Correcting Common Nutrient Deficiencies

Soil pH will affect the availability of nutrients. If you see symptoms such as the ones indicated below, test the soil pH to see if it needs adjusting before adding fertilizer. Between pH 6.5 and 7.0 all nutrients in the soil are sufficiently available to plants.

Nutrient	Natural Sources	Role in Plant Growth	Deficiency Symptoms	How to Correct Deficiency
Nitrogen (N)	Organic matter, legumes.	In moderate amounts, promotes sturdy growth, especially in leaves and stems.	Entire plant is pale green or yellowish. Older leaves lose green color first. Growth is reduced. Leaves and branches are smaller and fewer. Fall color shows early.	Use a complete fertilizer; add high-nitrogen materials, such as blood meal; add organic matter. Nitrogen is used up or leached out quickly, so apply moderate amounts through the growing season.
Phosphorus (P)	Soil, organic matter.	Stimulates root branching and production of root hairs; helps plants mature more rapidly.	Leaves become very dark green; undersides turn red to bronze. Purple to reddish color may show in leaf veins and stems, especially on younger plants.	Use a complete fertilizer, bone meal, or rock or colloidal phosphate. Mix into the top 6 to 8 inches of soil so it is accessible to roots.
Potassium (K)	Soil.	Has several important functions in cell metabolism, protein synthesis, and water retention.	Lower leaves turn yellow or brown along edges and between veins. Leaves may crinkle and roll upward. Stems are weak and tend to wilt. Disease resistance is lowered. Yield and quality of flowers and fruit are reduced.	Use a complete fertilizer, greensand, wood ash, or langbeinite (which also supplies sulfur and magnesium). Potassium leaches most readily in light, sandy soil, so you may need to reapply fairly often.

lowed by phosphorus, then potassium. A fertilizer with a 5-10-5 ratio, for example, contains 5 percent by weight of nitrogen, 10 percent phosphate (a form of phosphorus), and 5 percent potash (a form of potassium). The balance of the material consists of fillers (to add bulk for easier spreading) or of other elements in compounds with nitrogen, phosphorus, and potassium that are not immediately available to plants. Natural organic fertilizers contain significant amounts of nutrients that are released gradually to plants and fall in this latter group. A general complete fertilizer is suitable for a wide range of flowering and vegetable garden plants. There also are fertilizer products specially formulated for particu-

Nutrient	Natural Sources	Role in Plant Growth	Deficiency Symptoms	How to Correct Deficiency
Sulfur (S)	Soil, rain.	Helps synthesize protein.	Entire plant (both older and younger leaves) has a yellow cast. Growth is reduced.	Use flowers of sulfur (elemental sulfur), gypsum (also supplies calcium), or langbeinite (also supplies potassium and magnesium).
Calcium (Ca)	Limestone, soil, organic matter.	Is required for cell division, hydration, and expansion.	Shoot tips are stunted and may die back. Young leaves may be small and distorted, with hooked tips. Flower petals may wilt even with adequate soil moisture.	Use ground limestone if you also need to raise soil pH. If pH is between 6.5 and 7.0, add gypsum (also supplies sulfur). Calcium tends to leach quickly from sandy soil.
Magnesium (Mg)	Soil, dolomitic limestone.	The central atom in the chlorophyll molecule and essential to life.	Lower leaves turn yellow between veins; may also turn yellow along the edges after initial red color develops. Leaf margins usually do not turn brown. Shoot growth is relatively normal until deficiency is severe.	Use dolomitic limestone (which also supplies calcium) if you also need to raise soil pH; otherwise use magnesium sulfate (Epsom salts) or langbeinite (also supplies sulfur and potassium).
Iron (Fe)	Soil.	Helps chlorophyll production; plays a role in respiration.	Symptoms show only on young leaves; no initial stunting or dieback. Young leaves and shoots turn yellow to almost white with severe deficiency; narrow strip of green shows along veins. Older leaves remain green. Shoots are normal in length, but diameter is reduced.	May be present but not available in soils with pH above 7; try lowering soil pH with sulfur. If that doesn't work, spray the foliage or amend the soil with an iron chelate.

Fertilizing Container Plants

Since the roots of container-grown plants can't spread far in search of nutrients, regular fertilizing is critical to keep them looking their best. Not only do potted plants quickly deplete the available nutrients, regular watering also washes nutrients away from the root zone. Adding compost, garden soil, and/or organic fertilizers to the growing medium at planting time will provide a small but steady supply of nutrients over time. But regular doses of liquid fertilizer will help meet your plants' nutrient needs when they are growing vigorously, keeping them lush and free-flowering.

Commercial liquid organic fertilizers, such as fish emulsion or seaweed extract, are convenient and easy to prepare; simply dilute and apply according to the directions on the label. If you'd rather make your own liquid fertilizer, see "Making Compost Tea" on page 93. Apply the fertilizer with a watering can to drench the roots or use a sprayer to mist the leaves. Start feeding about two weeks after planting, and feed every two weeks thereafter. If the plants are growing too rampantly, cut back to every three to four weeks; feed more often if plants look as if they need a boost. Stop fertilizing potted perennials, shrubs, and trees after midsummer so that they won't be encouraged to produce tender new growth that might be damaged by early frosts.

lar plants, such as roses or bulbs, which provide the ideal balance of nitrogen, phosphorus, and potassium to meet their special needs.

Some fertilizers provide only one or two of the three primary elements. Colloidal phosphate, for instance, usually has a ratio of 0-2-2, indicating that it provides phosphorus and potassium but not nitrogen. Blood meal usually has a ratio of 10-0-0, indicating that it supplies only nitrogen. These materials are useful if you know your soil is deficient in one or two nutrients. But you won't want to use them regularly, as you may end up with an excess of those nutrients, which can harm your plants.

Organic and Inorganic. As you read the fertilizer bags, keep in mind that "organic" and "inorganic" do not always mean the same thing as "natural" and "synthetic." Organic fertilizers are simply those derived from plant or animal residues or by-products, while inorganic fertilizers come from nonliving sources—rocks as well as chemical salts. Natural fertilizers are derived from natural sources (such as mineral deposits or animal by-products), while synthetic fertilizers are those processed in chemical plants. Read labels carefully to be sure you are buying a natural organic product. One clue is recognizable ingredients such as fish meal, blood meal, or bone meal. Many products also state that they are specifically recommended for organic gardens.

Gardeners who manage their plantings organically use only fertilizers made from natural materials such as manure, bone meal, and wood ash and from inorganic compounds mined from natural deposits. These natural inorganic compounds, such as rock phosphate, limestone, greensand, and granite meal, are used in the same chemical form in which they are mined and are therefore acceptable to organic gardeners. The rock must be ground into a very fine powder before being sold for use as fertilizer, however. Plants absorb *all* of their nutrients in the form of inorganic ions (the result of the nutrient source dissolving in water). Whether these ions come from an organic source such as cow manure or fish meal, from a natural inorganic source such as lime or rock phosphate, or from a synthetic chemical fertilizer makes no difference in the effect they have on a plant.

Although the nutrients in fertilizers formulated from natural sources and those in fertilizers synthesized in a chemical factory are absorbed by plants in exactly the same form, natural organic materials have several advantages over synthetic compounds. In natural organic fertilizers most of the nutrients have to be broken down by soil organisms and thus are released slowly, usually over a period of months or years. This makes them safer to use, as they are less likely to burn plant roots, and they are less likely to be lost by leaching. Natural fertilizers and amendments also help improve the soil and/or feed soil organisms, and they don't discourage earthworm activity, as the salts in synthetic fertilizers do. On the downside, you can't easily predict how fast the nutrients in an organic fertilizer will be available to your plants, because the speed of breakdown depends upon several factors, including pH, temperature, and moisture levels. But with some experience, and with the help of regular soil tests, you can provide a steady supply of nutrients using organic fertilizers.

Natural organic fertilizers contain varying amounts of plant nutrients. Most gardeners use the bulkier materials, including manures, compost, and other plant and animal residues, primarily as amendments—materials that feed the soil and improve its physical structure. They value the organic matter in these materials more than their nutrient content. Manure, compost, and other bulky substances can be difficult to spread uniformly, and the nutrients they contain are not available to plants until soil organisms have broken down the material. For this reason they are best added to the soil for long-term improvement rather than as a short-term feeding fix.

Other organic materials, including bone meal, blood meal, dried sewage sludge, and fish emulsion, make excellent nutrient sources. These materials are dried and pulverized or processed before they are packaged as fertilizers. (Some animal manures are treated this way as well.) The main use of these materials is to supply nutrients rather than to condition the soil.

Granular and Liquid Fertilizers. When buying fertilizers, you'll also need to consider whether to buy them in liquid or solid (usually granular) form. Most of the time, solid fertilizers are the practical choice, as they are easy to apply and give relatively long-lasting results (usually over a period of months). But liquids, such as fish emulsion, or powders, such as kelp meal, both of which are designed to be dissolved in water, can be an excellent choice if you need fast results; the nutrients are already dissolved in liquid, and plants can absorb what they need immediately. This is a real plus if your plants are already showing symptoms of nutrient deficiencies or if your annual flowers and vegetable plants need a midseason boost to promote more flowers and fruit. Homemade compost and manure teas also give plants a liquid fertilizer boost—see "Making Compost Tea" on page 93. Liquid fertilizers are also useful for container plantings. The effect won't be long-lasting, though—maybe only a few weeks—so don't rely on liquids to supply all your plants' needs. You'll get the best results by adding solid fertilizers to your soil and saving the liquids for feeding container gardens and individual plants.

Reading Fertilizer Labels. You'll find a wealth of information on the labels of packaged fertilizers. The concentrations of nutrients listed there are guaranteed by law. The analysis, or NPK, ratio of the material—that series of three numbers—is usually displayed quite prominently. These percentages represent the minimum concentration of an element that is immediately available to plants; the fertilizer usually contains a small amount more. The label also provides infor-

Feeding the soil with regular additions of compost and other organic matter may provide all the nutrients your plants need. Applying fertilizers is a good way to feed plants in a new garden, however, as part of an overall soil-building program. Regular feeding also boosts yields in the vegetable garden.

mation about the compounds used to supply the essential elements that are in the fertilizer. It should also state whether the fertilizer is organic or all natural.

If the nutrients in a fertilizer total less than 30 percent of its weight, it is classified as a low-analysis fertilizer; if more than 30 percent, it is a high-analysis fertilizer. A 10-20-10 fertilizer, for example, would have 40 percent nutrients, so it would be high analysis, while a 3-2-2, with a 7 percent nutrient content, would be low analysis. Synthetic fertilizers generally have high nutrient analyses; organic fertilizers, low ones. While low-analysis fertilizers tend to be more expensive, since you need to add more of them to get the same immediate benefit that a high-analysis material would supply, keep in mind that the analysis accounts only for the nutrients that are *readily available*. Low-analysis materials are usually derived from natural sources, so they rely on soil organisms to break them down and release all their nutrients, and this takes time. After a few years of adding natural fertilizers—and organic matter—to your soil, the nutrient levels will build up, and you may actually need to add less fertilizer in future years.

Common Fertilizer Materials

The following are some of the most common organic and inorganic natural fertilizers available. While some provide one nutrient, others provide the three major nutrients plus other minor nutrients and minerals.

Fertilizer	Average Analysis	Application Rate per 100 sq. ft.	Comments
Blood meal (dried blood)	10-0-0	1 to 3 lbs.	Organic, natural. Nitrogen is readily available; one application will last only 3 to 4 months.
Bone meal (steamed)	1-11-0	1 to 3 lbs.	Organic, natural. Also supplies calcium. Gradually raises soil pH.
Compost	1-1-1	1- to 2-in. layer.	Organic, natural. Actual nutrient content can vary widely, depending on ingredients. Also supplies organic matter.
Cow manure (dried)	2-2-2	10 to 20 lbs.	Organic, natural. Also supplies organic matter.
Fish emulsion	5-1-1	Follow label directions.	Organic, natural. Liquid. Nitrogen content can vary widely. Also contains many minerals. Pungent odor.
Fish meal	5-3-3	1 to 3 lbs.	Organic, natural. Also contains many minerals.
Horse manure (composted or dried)	2-1-2	10 to 20 lbs.	Organic, natural. Also supplies organic matter.
Kelp meal	2-1-3	1 to 2 lbs.	Organic, natural. Also supplies many "trace" minerals (nutrients that plants need in very small amounts).
Langbeinite	0-0-22	0.5 to 1 lb.	Inorganic, natural. Commonly sold as Sul-Po-Mag or K-Mag. Also supplies sulfur and magnesium.
Rock phosphate	0-3-0	2 to 4 lbs.	Inorganic, natural. Contains much more phosphorus than indicated, but releases the nutrient very slowly (over 3 to 4 years). Most effective on acid soil (pH 6.2 or below).
Wood ash (fresh)	0-1-8	2 lbs.	Organic, natural. Also supplies calcium. Apply every other fall; in spring, dig or till under. Raises soil pH; do not overuse it.

Some fertilizers can acidify your soil, and most labels indicate the product's potential effect on acidity. This is typically expressed as the amount of calcium carbonate (ground limestone) needed to neutralize the change in pH that a ton of fertilizer could cause. The higher this amount, the more acid your soil will become when you apply the fertilizer. For many soils, the small amount you'll be using in the garden won't cause any problems. But if your soil already has a low pH, you'll want to avoid fertilizers that can contribute to acidity.

APPLYING FERTILIZERS

When, how, and how much you fertilize will depend on the materials you've chosen and the plants you are growing. Your soil-test results will help you determine how much of each nutrient you need to add. Many commercial fertilizers include suggested application rates right on their label. And below you'll find out how to apply different forms of fertilizer. For more detailed information on tailoring your fertilizer program to your particular plantings, see chapter 6, "Soil Care for Garden Plants."

How Much to Apply. Once you have your soil-test results, you will need to figure out how much packaged fertilizer it will take to meet the lab's recommendations. This is relatively simple and requires only basic math. The example below will help you make the calculations you need.

Example. Your soil-test report recommends adding 2 pounds of nitrogen per 1,000 square feet. You are fertilizing 100 square feet with a 5-3-3 fertilizer. How much should you apply?

Start by figuring out how much 5 percent fertilizer it takes to supply 2 pounds of nitrogen to 1,000 square feet. Set up a simple equation, using x as the unknown amount of fertilizer:

$$0.05x = 2 \text{ lbs.}$$
$$x = 2 / 0.05$$
$$x = 40 \text{ lbs.}$$

It will take 40 pounds of a 5-3-3 fertilizer per 1,000 square feet to supply 2 pounds of nitrogen. Since you are fertilizing one-tenth that area, you need to spread 4 pounds of 5-3-3 to meet the lab's nitrogen recommendation.

Dry Fertilizers. Loose or granular fertilizers are easy to apply. To top-dress a small area, scatter the fertilizer evenly by hand, or use a mechanical spreader for larger areas, such as lawns. In unplanted areas, distribute the fertilizer over the surface as uniformly as you can and dig or till it into the soil. Around established plantings, rake off any existing mulch and scatter the fertilizer evenly over the soil near the drip line rather than around the stem of the plant. Then rake lightly to scratch it into the surface, and replace or add mulch if appropriate. Avoid getting dry fertilizer on plant leaves, as it can damage them.

During the growing season, vegetables and annuals are often fertilized by side-dressing. To use this technique, spread the fertilizer in a band along the rows—again, just outside the drip line of the plant, where the roots are most active. Then very carefully work it into the top few inches of soil. Be careful not to damage the roots in the process.

Applying Dry Fertilizer

It's easy to apply dry fertilizer: simply scatter it on the soil around established plants or spread it evenly over the soil before digging or tilling unplanted areas. Use the application rate suggested by your soil-test results or follow the instructions on the product label.

Applying Liquid Fertilizer

Apply liquid fertilizer by drenching the soil around the base of your plants or spraying it on their leaves. The roots or leaves will quickly absorb the nutrients.

Liquid Fertilizers. Effective and easy to use, soluble-powder and liquid fertilizers provide immediately available nutrients to your plants. Simply dissolve the specified amount of powder or liquid in a container of water, according to the package directions, then drench the soil around your plants with it. Apply enough solution to wet the soil down to the root depth (roughly 6 inches); using more will just waste fertilizer.

In small areas and containers, you can apply the fertilizer with a watering can. If you have a large garden, applying it with a garden hose is more practical. A hose-end sprayer, which mixes concentrated fertilizer with the spray of water, makes this task easier. Or, for more control over the concentration of fertilizer delivered, attach a metered siphoning device between the faucet and the hose. Go over the plants several times, directing the spray carefully to ensure even distribution. The nutrients that land on the leaves will be absorbed quickly, but most of the solution will end up on the soil surface. Therefore, water thoroughly when you've finished spraying, to help wash the nutrients down into the soil. Plan to make several applications during the growing season rather than supplying all of the nutrients at once. Too high a concentration at one time will damage leaves and stems.

CHAPTER 5
MAKING AND USING COMPOST

Composting is one of the best things you can do for your garden. Besides giving you a place to recycle garden and kitchen wastes (thereby keeping them out of landfills), a compost pile will provide you with one of the best soil-improving materials available—all for free. Worked into your soil or used as a mulch, compost improves soil structure while adding organic matter and nutrients. Once you get started composting, your only problem may be scrounging up the raw materials you need to create all the compost you want.

CHOOSING THE RIGHT SITE

While it's possible to compost successfully just about anywhere, here are a few pointers to keep in mind when selecting a site. First, it's usually best to locate the pile in an out-of-the-way spot. You want it to be convenient to your garden, but

Consider your neighbors when planning your composting system: nongardeners may see a highly visible compost pile as trash, not "gardener's gold." Putting compost in a simple cage or bin—or in an elaborate brick-and-wood bin like this—is a good solution for city gardeners.

Composting under Trees

In warm climates, consider locating a compost pile under a tree or in the shadow of a garage or other building. Shade helps prevent the pile from getting too hot and drying out too fast. Tree roots can quickly grow up into a ground-level pile, making it tough to remove the finished compost. To prevent this, build your pile on a wooden pallet or a base of rocks, poles, or timbers.

Homemade Compost Cages and Bins

To make a good-looking three-bin compost setup like this one, set 2-by-6s into the ground for the posts and make the sides from 1-by-6s. Build each bin at least 3 feet high, wide, and deep. On the front side of each bin, use 1-by-1s to make slots to hold the front slats. Spacers between the slats allow air to reach the pile. Make compost in one bin and turn it into the second one; use the third bin for stockpiling materials for the next batch.

It's easy to make a simple bin, 3 to 4 feet in diameter, from rabbit fencing or similar sturdy fencing with narrow openings. When you're ready to turn the pile, just unhook the wire and pull off the cage. A cage or bin can also be used to contain a cold-compost pile, which isn't turned.

you don't necessarily want to have it in full view, as even the best-maintained composting operation isn't especially attractive. Even if *you* don't mind it, consider that your neighbors may not appreciate looking at a pile of debris. Enclosing compost in bins or cages may help somewhat, but it's still worth selecting a spot that's not highly visible from your house or your neighbors' property. Putting up a fence or screen may be a help.

Ideally, the spot should be well-drained and level. In cool climates, a sunny spot will help keep your pile warm and promote faster breakdown. In warm climates, a slightly shady location will prevent overheating.

CONTAINING YOUR COMPOST

You can create great compost without an enclosure of any kind, but containing it has some advantages. Besides making the composting area look neater, cages, bins, and other enclosures help keep the material evenly moist, promoting faster decomposition. Enclosures also prevent loose materials from blowing away and keep animals from rooting around in your pile for kitchen scraps and other food items.

If you decide to use an enclosure, make it at least 3 feet long, wide, and high to get enough material for fast decomposition. (If space is limited or you aren't in a hurry for compost, you can get away with a smaller container; just don't expect the pile to heat up the way a larger batch would.) If possible, construct at least two enclosures. That way you can be filling one while the other is breaking down. As you gain experience, you may wish to add extra enclosures to hold finished compost or slow-to-decompose materials.

Cages. Garden centers, home centers, and garden supply catalogs usually offer several choices of cages to enclose compost piles. The cages may be square or round (either shape works fine), and they are relatively inexpensive and

> ### TIPS FOR SUCCESS
> #### PLAN AHEAD FOR COMPOST
>
> If you are planning to renovate an existing garden bed, consider using it as a temporary composting site. A cage works well for containing a temporary pile; simply place it in or next to the bed, ideally the year before you plan on renovating. Then make compost as you would at any other site. When you are ready to renovate, you'll have a convenient supply of finished compost. This technique also works well for extending a bed or planning for an entirely new one: simply make compost where you'll need it next. To hide the pile during the season, plant annual vines around the perimeter of the cage. Pole and runner beans work for this purpose, as do flowering vines such as morning glories.

Recycle kitchen wastes such as vegetable peelings, coffee grounds, eggshells, and old tea bags by adding them to the compost pile. Don't add animal products such as bones or fat, however. Compost is the best soil amendment of all—and it's free.

easy to put together. You can also make your own out of a length of wire-mesh fencing; simply fasten the two ends together with wire or heavy twine to create a broad cylinder and stand it on one end.

The closer together the wires are, the less likely compost materials are to fall out. If the wire isn't heavy enough to support itself, pound a few metal fence posts into the ground around the cage and fasten the wire to them. To reduce moisture loss in very hot weather, line wire cages with cardboard. When you are ready to turn or use your compost, it's easy to unfasten the cage for ready access.

Bins. Compost bins are more solid than cages and tend to be more permanent. Commercially produced bins are usually made of wood or plastic. You can also build your own from cement blocks, lumber, wooden pallets, or even brick (for a really classy compost corner). Just remember to leave one side open or hinged in such a way that you can easily reach the pile for turning or shoveling. A roof, to protect the pile from wind, sun, and rain, is a helpful feature, although not absolutely necessary.

Common Compost Ingredients

For best results when making compost, mix two to three parts of high-carbon materials with one part of high-nitrogen materials.

Material	Comments
Animal manures	Nitrogen source. Do not add dog or cat droppings to compost; they carry diseases that can affect humans.
Garden debris	Nitrogen source when fresh and green; high in carbon when dry. Do not add diseased material or weeds that have gone to seed. Shred or chop woody stems, tough stalks, and dense clumps before adding to hot compost.
Grass clippings	Nitrogen source. Mix well with other ingredients to prevent matting.
Hay and straw	Carbon source (fresh hay can contribute nitrogen as well). Decompose best if chopped before adding. Hay may contain weed and grass seeds.
Kitchen wastes	Nitrogen source (mostly). Vegetable trimmings, eggshells, and coffee grounds are excellent for compost. Do not add meat scraps, fat, or bones, which are slow to break down and can attract animals.
Leaves	Nitrogen source when fresh and green; carbon source when brown and dry. Deciduous leaves compost well; evergreen needles decompose slowly. Shred leaves before adding to pile to prevent them from forming a dense, impermeable layer.
Paper	Carbon source. Shred before adding. Some glossy color-printed paper contains potentially dangerous heavy metals; avoid it or mix with other papers to minimize the danger.
Sawdust and wood shavings	Carbon source. Hardwoods break down faster than softwoods (such as pine). Sawdust decomposes faster than wood shavings.
Sod	Nitrogen source. Great way to recycle sod removed from new garden areas. Place sod pieces upside down on the pile and turn often to encourage decomposition and discourage sprouting.

Trash-Can Composting. A large plastic garbage can with a lid can be handy for composting in a small area. This is an excellent setup if you compost lots of kitchen scraps through the winter, as the enclosure will minimize odor and keep animals out.

Trash-Can Composter

To make this simple setup, cut out the bottom of a large rubber or plastic trash container and poke or drill a dozen or so ¼- to ½-inch holes in the sides. Dig a hole about 1 foot deep and as wide as the base, then sink the bottom of the can into the hole. Replace the lid each time you add more scraps.

When adding fresh material to a trash-can composter, toss in a handful or two of the soil that you removed from the hole. Also add some dry leaves or shredded newspaper if the material is very moist, then replace the lid. (For winter composting, stockpile your leaves and other materials in plastic garbage bags in fall so they'll be available, rather than frozen into the ground, over the winter.) Earthworms will come up from the soil below the composter to break down the scraps. When the can is full, let it sit for several months until the materials in it are mostly unrecognizable; then lift the can to reach the finished compost. It's handy to have two cans, so you can fill one while the other is composting.

BUILDING YOUR COMPOST PILE

Composting can be as simple or as complex as you want to make it. If you aren't in a hurry for the finished product, you can take a simple, low-effort approach. But the more time and thought you put into it, the sooner you'll have top-quality compost to use in your garden.

Cold Compost. This system is the easiest of all: simply toss all your kitchen scraps, garden trimmings, and leaves in a pile and wait a year or two for them to break down. The resulting material will be rich in a variety of beneficial microorganisms, making it an excellent soil amendment.

Ideal Ingredients for Top-Quality Compost

Good raw materials for compost include grass clippings, vegetable peelings, eggshells, coffee grounds, soft plant trimmings, and fallen leaves.

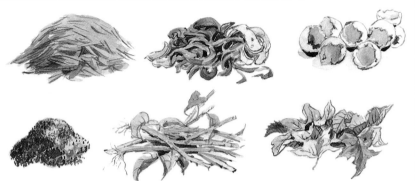

Keep These Out of Your Compost

Materials that don't belong in a compost pile include bones, fat, and meat scraps, which will attract animals. Also avoid adding diseased plants from the garden, weeds with seeds, and woody prunings.

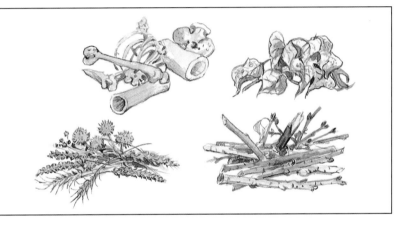

This method may be a good choice if you have plenty of room to create piles and let them sit for a few years to break down. It's not necessary to turn the piles, but doing so once or twice a year will help the materials decompose more evenly.

Hot Compost. There's no question that hot composting takes more time and energy, but in return, you'll have finished material in three months or less. (The heat in a hot compost pile is generated by microorganisms busily breaking down materials.) Another advantage of hot composting is that you can compost roughly three times the amount of material in the same amount of space each year, so you'll need less space and you'll get more compost. Some gardeners also find hot composting to be a lot of fun, as they tinker with their piles to get just the right balance of materials for fast heating and decomposing.

Homemade Compost Sifter

To make a simple sifter for compost, staple or nail a piece of $1/4$- to $1/2$-inch-mesh hardware cloth to a frame of 2-by-4s. Lay the finished screen over your wheelbarrow, toss on a shovelful of compost, and stir it with your shovel or shake the screen to sift out the lumps. If your compost is too chunky to sift easily, try shredding it first, or let it decompose for a few more weeks.

Each hot compost pile you build will be a little different, because you'll probably have different materials available through the seasons. But whatever you use, the principles remain the same. Mixing a balance of high-carbon and high-nitrogen materials is the key to fast decomposition. High-carbon materials tend to be brown and dry—examples include fallen leaves, straw, and sawdust. High-nitrogen ingredients are often green and moist—think of grass clippings, vegetable peelings, and fresh garden trimmings.

A general rule of thumb for building a compost pile is to mix two to three parts of high-carbon (brown and dry) materials with one part of high-nitrogen (green and moist) materials. You can build the pile in alternating layers—for example, a 2- to 3-inch layer of dead leaves, topped with 1 inch of grass clippings, then 2 to 3 more inches of leaves, then 1 inch of horse manure, and so on. Or just mix the materials as you go—two or three forkfuls of leaves, one of grass clippings, two or three of straw, and so forth, all mixed with the fork as you construct the pile. This balance of brown-and-dry and green-and-moist provides the nutrients the microorganisms need to multiply, allowing them to quickly decompose materials into finished compost. Chopping or shredding leaves, straw, and other ingredients before adding them to the pile speeds up the process by giving the microorganisms more surfaces to work on.

It's best to build a hot compost pile all at one time, so stockpile materials until you have enough to build a whole pile. Make the base of the pile roughly 4 feet square and taper the sides a bit as you work upward so that the top is roughly 3 feet square. The finished pile should be *at least* 3 feet deep. You can make the

Composting systems can be as simple as a pile of garden clippings and kitchen wastes in an out-of-the-way corner of the yard. A more elaborate operation, like this three-bin system, is designed to produce quantities of compost for a large garden.

For a rustic look that's neater than an open pile, consider corralling your compost with logs.

Troubleshooting Compost Problems

Making compost is generally a trouble-free activity, but you may encounter one or more of the problems listed below.

Problem	Solution
Pile has offensive odor.	An ammonia-like odor indicates that the pH is too high, probably from the action of animal, particularly poultry, manures or from overuse of lime. Biological activity should eventually cause pH to drop and reduce odor; turning the pile and adding more plant residues may speed the process. Next time use less manure. Other odors usually mean the pile is too wet. Turn it, mixing in dry leaves, chopped straw, or shredded paper.
Pile attracts flies and gnats.	The pile is probably too wet and generating odors that attract these pests. Turn the pile, mixing in some dry material. If you are composting lots of kitchen scraps, use a closed composting container, such as a bin or covered garbage can.
Pile does not heat up at all.	Probably means an imbalance of carbon and nitrogen. Materials may take a year or two to break down; for faster decomposition, mix in more high-nitrogen materials. Or pile may be too wet or too dry. If wet, turn it, mixing in dry material. If too dry, fluff pile with a pitchfork and spray with water.
Pile heats up only slightly.	If pile is less than 3 feet on each side, it is too small; add more material. Otherwise turn the pile and mix in more high-nitrogen material.
Pile heats properly, but there is a whitish material under the surface.	Pile is too dry. The whitish deposit is a sign of actinomycetes, which are more tolerant of dry conditions than are other organisms. Turn the pile and add water.
Finished compost contains chunks of undecomposed material.	Sift out the larger chunks and add them to another pile; use the rest of the finished compost as usual. Next time, chop or shred tough, fibrous materials before adding.
Unwanted seedlings sprout where finished compost is used as mulch.	After weeding, cover compost with another mulch to discourage further sprouting. Use the rest of that batch as a soil amendment (dig or till into the soil) instead of mulch. In future, avoid adding plant tops that have gone to seed. Even composted tomatoes can leave many viable seeds.

pile bigger if you wish, but don't make it much smaller, or it won't have enough material to heat up properly. As you construct the pile, spray it with water periodically unless the materials you are using are already very wet. The finished pile should feel lightly moist to the touch—like a damp sponge—but it shouldn't drip if you squeeze a handful. If your pile is too wet, it won't heat properly because the microorganisms in the pile can't get enough oxygen, and you'll need to mix in more dry material. It's easier to skimp a bit on the water while you're building the pile and add more later, if needed.

Within a day or two, you should be able to feel the pile growing warm if you work your hand toward the center. After a few more days, you'll feel the warmth when you touch the outside of the pile, and you may notice the pile steaming on cool mornings. Check the pile every few days to monitor the temperature and moisture. When the pile begins to cool off, or when it feels dry (usually after a few weeks), it's time to turn it. Build a new pile next to the old one, placing the material that was near the surface of the old pile in the middle of the new one. Add water if needed. The temperature should rise as it did in the first pile. When the pile cools off again and the center is just warm, you can use the compost then or turn it again and let it sit until you are ready for it. By this time your pile will have shrunk to half or less of its original volume.

Hot composting is as much an art as a science, so you'll find ways to fine-tune your technique as you gain experience. Some gardeners like to use a special compost thermometer to more accurately monitor temperature changes. You can find these thermometers in some garden centers and garden supply catalogs for around fifteen dollars.

Another handy tool is a compost aerator, which looks something like a walking stick with two hinged flaps at the end. You poke this end deep into the pile,

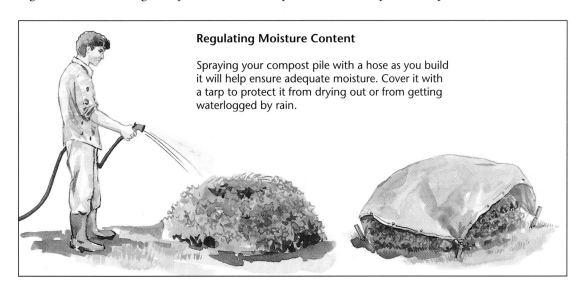

Regulating Moisture Content

Spraying your compost pile with a hose as you build it will help ensure adequate moisture. Cover it with a tarp to protect it from drying out or from getting waterlogged by rain.

and as you pull it back, the flaps open. This helps to mix the ingredients and lets needed air into the middle, speeding up decomposition without your having to turn the pile. (Using this tool also will speed up the action of a cold compost pile that you don't intend to turn.) You may also find it helpful to cover your compost pile with a plastic tarp while it "cooks." This will help hold in moisture during dry spells and prevent rain from getting the pile too wet.

Using Compost

Compost is ready to use when it is dark and crumbly, with the original ingredients mostly unrecognizable. It's fine if there are still some lumps, especially if you plan to work the compost into the soil. If you have numerous large lumps, or if you want a fine, uniform material for mulching, sift your compost through a wire screen to remove the chunks and toss them into a new pile. See the illustration on page 88 for information on making a simple compost sifter.

Using Compost as Mulch

Rake or scoop the existing mulch from the base of the plant, spread a $1/2$- to 1-inch layer of compost over the soil, then replace the mulch. Avoid adding compost around shrubs and trees after midsummer.

Making Compost Tea

Your plants will enjoy a dose of compost in liquid form. To make compost tea, place a shovelful of finished compost in a burlap sack or old pillowcase, tie the top closed, and let it soak in a tub or large bucket of water for several days. When the water looks dark, remove the "tea bag" and toss the sodden compost onto a new pile. Add water to dilute the remaining liquid to the color of weak tea. You can use the same process to make manure tea.

Apply the liquid to the soil with a watering can or spray it on the leaves. (Strain compost or manure tea through pantyhose or other fine mesh before putting it in a sprayer.) A dose of compost or manure tea once or twice a summer is ideal for giving your plants, especially those in containers, a gentle nutrient boost. As with a compost mulch, don't use compost or manure tea on perennials, shrubs, or trees after midsummer.

If you are using compost to add organic matter to your soil, spread it evenly over the soil surface, then dig or till it into the topsoil. A layer 1 to 2 inches thick is great, if you have that much compost; if not, even $1/4$ to $1/2$ inch can help. If you are working with fairly chunky compost, work it into the soil in fall to give it more time to break down. Spring application is fine for compost that is mostly crumbly.

A 1- to 3-inch layer of compost makes a great nutrient-rich mulch for vegetables, flowers, shrubs, and trees. If you don't have enough compost to mulch that thickly, spread a $1/2$- to 1-inch layer and top that with another mulch, such as shredded bark or chopped leaves. Late spring and fall are good times to mulch with compost. Summer mulching is fine for annuals and vegetables, but avoid adding fresh compost mulch around perennials, shrubs, and trees after midsummer. Because the compost releases nutrients, it can encourage a spurt of late-season growth that may be damaged by early frosts.

CHAPTER 6

SOIL CARE FOR GARDEN PLANTS

Building great soil is an important step in creating a healthy, beautiful, easy-care garden. While the soil-care basics covered in previous chapters will produce good results in all parts of your garden, you can try some special tricks to fine-tune your soil-building efforts for particular kinds of plants. By tailoring your soil preparation, mulching, and fertilizing techniques, you will give all your plants the best possible growing conditions. They'll respond by performing better than you would ever imagine. An added benefit is that healthy, vigorous plants are not as prone to disease and pest problems as those growing in less-than-ideal conditions. You'll also save money, because you won't be wasting your gardening budget on expensive fertilizers that your plants may not need.

ANNUALS

Annuals need plenty of nutrients to produce leafy growth, flower prolifically, and set seed within one growing season. While the needs of individual plants differ,

---

The basic principles of soil care are the same regardless of what you grow, but the techniques vary. With perennials, it pays to prepare the soil deeply and add plenty of organic matter when the bed is first planted, because the plants stay in the same spot for a number of years.

annuals as a group tend to thrive in loose, well-dug soil that is rich in organic matter and has an ample supply of nutrients and moisture. Fortunately, it's not difficult to provide these conditions, because you have a chance to improve the soil every year as you prepare the planting site.

Preparing the Soil. Annuals tend to be fairly shallow-rooted, concentrating most of their growth in the top 6 inches or so of soil. But within this space, the plants produce masses of fine, many-branched roots to search out the nutrients and moisture needed for fast growth and flowering. While annuals certainly grow well in deeply worked soil, you can get excellent results by loosening only the top 6 to 8 inches of the planting area. If your soil is particularly rocky, wet, compacted, or otherwise difficult to dig, loosen the existing soil as much as you can, then build a raised bed filled with 4 to 6 inches of good-quality topsoil over the site.

The first spring, spread a 1- to 2-inch layer of finished compost and scatter a balanced garden fertilizer (applied according to label directions) over the site. Then dig or till these materials into the soil. Rake the surface to break up lumps and remove rocks and other debris, then plant or sow as usual. At the end of the grow-

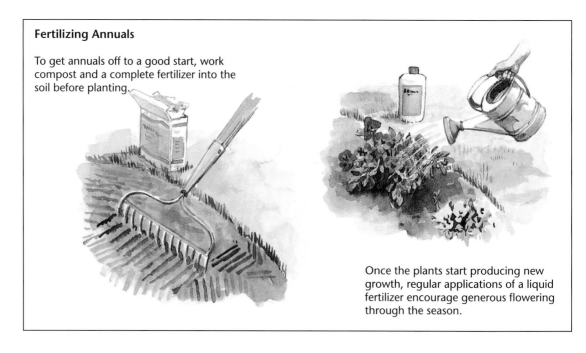

Fertilizing Annuals

To get annuals off to a good start, work compost and a complete fertilizer into the soil before planting.

Once the plants start producing new growth, regular applications of a liquid fertilizer encourage generous flowering through the season.

Many annuals are heavy feeders and have fine, heavily branched roots in the top few inches of soil. They don't need deep soil preparation like perennials, but compost worked into the surface along with a balanced organic fertilizer gets them off to a good start.

ing season, pull out the plants (roots and all) and toss them onto the compost pile. Then spread a 2- to 3-inch layer of chunky, nearly finished compost over the area to protect the soil over the winter. In spring, dig or till the remaining material into the soil along with more balanced garden fertilizer, then rake and plant.

Mulching. A relatively fine-textured organic mulch, such as finished compost, cocoa shells, or finely shredded bark, is ideal for annuals. It helps retain moisture and suppress weeds while the annuals fill in, then breaks down by the end of the growing season, releasing nutrients and adding organic matter to the soil.

If you grow annuals from seeds sown directly in the garden, wait until the seedlings are 3 to 4 inches tall before mulching to avoid smothering the small plants. If you set out transplants, you can mulch immediately after planting and watering. A 1- to 2-inch layer works best in most conditions, but if slugs are a major problem, consider starting with just $1/4$ to $1/2$ inch, then adding more as the plants grow bigger and the weather gets drier. As you spread the mulch, keep it at least 1 inch away from plant stems to minimize the chance of rot.

Fertilizing. Working a balanced garden fertilizer into the soil at planting time goes a long way toward meeting the nutrient needs of annuals through the growing season. Keep in mind that fertilizers need to break down and dissolve in the soil water before your plants can use them, however, and with organic-based fertilizers, this may take a few weeks. This may be fine for direct-sown seedlings, which don't require lots of nutrients right away. Transplants, on the other hand, benefit from a dose of liquid nutrients just after planting to support strong root and top growth. Mix a solution of seaweed (kelp) extract according to the package directions, or home-brew some compost tea, according to the directions in "Making Compost Tea" on page 93. (It's especially important to dilute the compost tea to a pale brown color for this use, as a too-strong tea can "burn" the soft, succulent growth on young plants.) Water the transplants with either liquid after planting. An additional dose of liquid fertilizer every six weeks will help keep annuals in peak condition and extend flowering into late summer and early fall.

If your fertilized plants show lots of lush, green growth but few or no flowers, they may be getting too much nitrogen. Avoid adding any additional fertilizer for at least several weeks, until you start seeing a better balance of leafy growth and flowers. It's also best to stop fertilizing during very hot weather, as many annuals naturally produce fewer flowers or none in response to the heat. When the weather cools off a bit and growth resumes, start fertilizing again.

PERENNIALS AND BULBS

Unlike annuals, perennial plants grow in the same spot for several years, so you have only one chance every few years, when you divide them, to make significant soil improvements. In the meantime, you need to rely on mulching and fertilizing to keep plants in top shape.

Preparing the Soil. Perennials tend to produce more extensive root systems than annuals, so they'll appreciate the extra effort you put into soil improvement before planting. Bulbs, which don't spread their roots as extensively, also grow

Before planting perennials, bulbs, trees, or shrubs, it pays to have the soil tested. Then you can add necessary amendments and adjust the pH as recommended in the test results.

best in well-prepared soil. It's smart to start with a soil test, so you can add lime, phosphorus, or other needed fertilizers and amendments before planting. Preparing a new planting site in fall is great if you can do it (it's essential for planting spring-blooming bulbs such as daffodils and tulips), because the amendments and organic matter have a chance to start breaking down before spring planting.

In sandy soils, thoroughly loosening the top 8 inches or so is enough. Spreading a 2-inch layer of organic matter over the area before digging helps enrich the soil and increase its moisture-holding capacity. This is also the time to add a scattering of balanced garden fertilizer (according to the rate recommended on the label), unless your soil-test results indicate that you need to correct a specific nutrient imbalance. Organic matter gets used up quickly in the well-aerated conditions of sandy soil, so for the longest-lasting benefit, apply roughly half of it as a fine-textured material, such as finished compost, and the rest as a coarser, longer-lasting material, such as pine bark.

If your soil is on the clay side, digging deeply will greatly improve rooting conditions. Yes, digging this heavier soil can be hard work, but the results last for years, and the extra effort pays off. (Deep-digging also benefits sandy soil, as it gives you a chance to work extra organic matter into the area.) To get down deep, spread a 1-inch layer of organic matter and a scattering of fertilizer (as recommended above for sandy soil) over the site, then dig a trench about 8 inches deep and 1 foot wide along one edge of the planting area. Pile the removed soil on a tarp or in a wheelbarrow. Spread a 1-inch layer of compost or other organic matter over the bottom of the trench, then work it into the soil with a spading fork. Working backward over the area (so you're not stepping on already loosened soil), dig another trench next to the first, turning the soil into the previous trench, then adding more organic matter and forking it into the bottom of the new trench. Continue this process until you reach the other end of the area, then fill the last trench with the soil you removed from the first one.

Mulching. Applying an organic mulch around perennials and bulbs helps keep the soil in shape after the initial planting season. A layer of fine-textured material, such as finished compost, topped with a coarser material, like shredded bark, provides the most benefit, but a 1- to 3-inch layer of just about any attractive organic mulch works well. The first year, apply the mulch right after planting and watering; in following years, wait until late spring, when the soil has warmed up and dried out a bit. Remember to leave a 2- to 3-inch-wide mulch-free zone around the base of each plant to prevent excess moisture from collecting around the crown and promoting rot.

At the end of the growing season, it's a good idea to rake off any remaining mulch and pile it along the edges of the bed. This discourages voles, mice, and other animal pests from making their winter homes in your garden. (These critters find plump perennial crowns and roots and fleshy bulbs to be tasty winter food.) Once the ground has frozen, these pests will have found homes elsewhere, so you can rake the mulches back over the bed to protect your soil.

Fertilizing. The best time to improve soil fertility is when you're preparing the site for planting, by adding plenty of organic matter along with any fertilizers and amendments recommended by your soil-test results. Working these materials into the soil distributes them evenly through the root zone.

Deep-Digging a Perennial Garden

A well-worked planting bed will provide ideal rooting conditions for perennials. To deep-dig, or double-dig, a perennial garden, first spread compost and fertilizer over the site, then dig a 1-foot-wide trench along one side, piling the soil on a tarp or in a wheelbarrow.

Spread more compost in the trench, then work it into the lower soil with a spading fork.

Repeat the process, turning the soil from the next trench into the previous one, until you reach the other side of the bed. Refill the last trench with the soil you removed from the first one.

After the first year, you'll have to rely on surface applications of solid or liquid fertilizers to supply needed nutrients. Each spring, apply a scattering of balanced garden fertilizer (follow the suggested application rate on the label) around perennials and bulbs. Lightly scratch it into the soil with a hand fork, taking care not to damage shallow roots or emerging stems.

A dose of liquid fertilizer helps newly planted perennials get off to a great start and gives established plants a welcome nutrient boost. Mix seaweed (kelp) extract or fish emulsion according to the label directions, or make your own liquid fertilizer by soaking finished compost in water. (See "Making Compost Tea" on page 93 for directions.) Using a watering can, drench the soil around the base of each plant with the fertilizer. An additional dose every four to six weeks, applied to the soil or sprayed on the leaves, encourages vigorous growth, but be sure to stop fertilizing by midsummer (roughly mid-July, or a few weeks later in warm climates). Otherwise your plants will keep producing lush new growth that may be damaged, or even killed, by cold spells in early fall.

Preventing Compaction in a Flower Garden

If you can't easily reach all parts of your garden from the edge, add steppingstones so you won't have to walk on the loosened soil.

Raised beds, such as these wood-framed ones, are ideal for growing vegetables in a site with poor soil. Paths between the beds facilitate caring for and harvesting crops. Paths should be at least wide enough for a wheelbarrow—wider if you use a garden cart.

VEGETABLES

Good soil care is probably more important in your vegetable garden than in any other part of your yard. Ornamental shrubs, trees, and flowers can often get by without regular fertilizing or special soil preparation, especially if you choose plants that are adapted to your natural soil conditions and climate. And yes, some vegetables will grow adequately without special attention to your soil. But if you put some extra effort into building your soil and supplying needed nutrients, you'll be rewarded with high yields of top-quality produce. And that's what you're planting vegetables for, isn't it?

Preparing the Soil. High yields start with good soil preparation. As soon as you choose a site—ideally the fall before planting—take a soil sample and check its pH and nutrient content, either with a home soil-test kit or through a lab. A pH of 6.5 to 7.2 suits the widest range of vegetable crops. If your soil's pH is higher or lower, your test results will help you determine how much sulfur or lime you need to add to adjust the pH. The test report will also help you determine if your soil has the necessary nutrients. If some nutrients are lacking or out of balance, you may need to add fertilizers to correct the problem.

One session of deep-digging when you start a new vegetable garden will benefit your plants for years to come. See the directions under "Perennials and Bulbs" for digging clay soils, page 100.

Deep-digging provides a loose, well-drained, organic-rich layer of soil that's easy for roots to grow through, so your plants can produce extensive root systems to support vigorous top growth, flowering, and fruiting. But what if your soil is just too hard, rocky, or wet to dig that deeply? Raised beds are an excellent solution. Loosening the soil as much as you can, then dumping more good-quality, rock-free soil on top of it will give you a well-drained rooting zone. A bed that's raised 4 to 6 inches above the normal soil surface is fine for most vegetables. You can make the beds higher, of course, but they may tend to dry out quickly, so you'll need to water them more often. It's a good idea to frame the sides of any raised bed with cement blocks, 2-by-6s, or landscape timbers of naturally rot-resistant wood to hold the soil in place.

After the first year, you'll need to loosen only the top 6 to 8 inches of soil before planting. Spread a 1- to 2-inch layer of finished compost or other organic matter over the site, then add any materials recommended on your soil-test results or a scattering of balanced garden fertilizer, according to the rate suggested on the label. Dig or till these materials into the soil, rake the surface to remove any rocks and debris, and you're ready to plant.

If your supply of compost and other organic matter is limited, a vegetable garden is a great place to take advantage of green manure crops, such as winter wheat or a legume like sweet clover. Plant these crops in early fall, then work the top growth and roots into the soil at least two weeks before spring planting. Besides adding generous amounts of organic matter, a fall cover crop protects your soil from erosion and compaction over the winter. Green manure crops can also be planted under established plants, such as tomatoes, as a ground cover or can fol-low crops in a rotation; a spring crop of lettuce can be followed by a green manure crop in a bed that needs improvement, for example. Any way you use them, be sure to turn the plants under before they set seed. For more information on green manures, see "Growing Your Own Soil Amendments" on page 30.

Mulching. A number of organic mulches work well in the vegetable garden. Compost, grass clippings, and other fine-textured materials are ideal because they

Feeding Vegetables with Green Manure Crops

A green manure or cover crop is an excellent way to add organic matter and nutrients to your vegetable garden soil. Sow the crop immediately after harvest and let it produce top growth.

In spring, mow or cut down the stems to chop them up a bit, then dig or till the tops and roots into the soil. Wait several weeks before planting to give the organic matter a chance to break down.

break down fairly quickly, releasing nutrients and organic matter to benefit your fast-growing crops. Hay and straw mulches are also excellent mulches for the vegetable garden. Hay tends to drop weed and grass seeds, but keeping a thick layer of hay on the soil at all times should smother any seeds that do reach the ground and germinate.

If you sow vegetable seeds directly into the garden, wait until the seedlings are 3 to 4 inches tall before mulching to avoid smothering the young sprouts. When you set out transplants, you can mulch right after planting and watering. Start with a 1- to 2-inch layer of fine-textured material or 6 to 8 inches of hay or straw. Check the depth of your mulch every four to eight weeks, and add more if needed to maintain the proper depth. Remember to keep mulch at least 1 or 2 inches away from plant stems to discourage rot from developing.

Fertilizing. Effective fertilizing begins with a soil test. Knowing what your soil has to start with is the only precise way to know what to add. For the very best harvests, it's even possible to tailor your fertilizer applications to the requirements of particular plants. For instance, lettuce, spinach, and other leafy crops benefit from extra nitrogen, while onions, leeks, and garlic benefit from extra phosphorus and potassium. Heavy feeders, such as cucumbers, melons, and cabbage-family plants (cabbage, broccoli, cauliflower, Brussels sprouts), appreciate extra doses of a balanced fertilizer through the season; carrots, peas, peppers, and radishes tend to be light feeders and will do fine with one initial fertilizing and a generous compost mulch.

If you haven't taken a soil test, or if you don't want to fuss with special fertilizers for particular crops, you can simply follow a general fertilizing program. Add a balanced garden fertilizer when you prepare the soil, then mulch with compost to provide a small but steady supply of extra nutrients through the season. In midsummer, again scatter a balanced fertilizer (according to the application rate on the label), and lightly scratch it into the mulch and soil around your plants. Or use a monthly application of liquid fertilizer instead. Use a commercial seaweed (kelp) extract or fish emulsion diluted according to the label directions, or make your own liquid fertilizer from finished compost (see "Making Compost Tea" on page 93). Apply the liquid with a watering can to drench the soil at the base of each plant or spray it on the leaves.

HERBS

Herbs are often grouped with vegetables in garden care recommendations, but many herbs actually have very different soil needs. Annual herbs, such as basil, are easy to accommodate in the vegetable garden and don't interfere with annual cycles of soil improvement, cover crops, or crop rotations. They also can be planted in a separate herb garden or spotted among perennial plantings. Perennial herbs such as lavender, thyme, and sage, however, are best planted with other perennials or in a garden of their own. That's because managing the soil in a vegetable garden is more difficult when you have to dig or till around perennials—and the perennials don't appreciate it either. In any case, it's worth treating herbs separately when considering their soil-care needs.

Raised Beds for Herbs

Raised beds provide the excellent drainage many herbs need to thrive. They are especially useful if your soil tends to be soggy or if cool, wet weather is common in your area.

Preparing the Soil. Most herbs grow just fine in well-drained garden soil with average fertility and a pH between 6.5 and 7.0. (Rich soil actually reduces the flavor and aroma of some herbs.) Deep-digging when you prepare the planting site, as you would for vegetables, will ensure good drainage, but it's not necessary. Loosening the top 4 to 6 inches of soil by digging or tilling will provide good growing conditions for most herbs. They'll benefit from having some organic matter worked into the soil, but they don't need as much as vegetables; a layer $\frac{1}{2}$ to 1 inch thick is fine.

Excellent drainage is critical for most herbs. If you know that your soil tends to be on the wet side, even if only at certain times of the year, consider installing raised beds, as discussed in "Preparing the Soil" for vegetables on page 104. Framing the beds with low walls of loose or mortared rocks makes them look attractive and complements the plants.

Mulching. A $\frac{1}{2}$- to 1-inch layer of finished compost will slowly release a small but steady supply of nutrients for your herbs. If you wish, you can top this with a thin layer of another mulch, such as shredded bark or pine needles. Just make sure you keep any mulch 2 to 3 inches away from the base of the stems; otherwise the extra moisture may cause the stems to rot. To further minimize the chance of rot, fill that mulch-free zone with a $\frac{1}{2}$- to 1-inch-deep ring of gravel to encourage good drainage around the stems.

If you sow herb seeds directly in the garden, wait until they are 3 to 4 inches tall before mulching, to avoid smothering the seedlings. You can mulch transplants right after planting and watering. Wait until late spring to mulch established perennial and shrubby herbs, to give the soil a chance to dry out and warm up a bit.

Fertilizing. Applying compost mulch yearly goes a long way toward meeting your herbs' nutrient needs. If you harvest frequently, though, they may benefit from a midsummer feeding. Scatter a balanced garden fertilizer over the planting, according to the application rate suggested on the label. Or give them a dose of liquid seaweed (kelp) extract or fish emulsion, diluted according to the label directions, or make your own liquid fertilizer by soaking compost in water (see "Making Compost Tea" on page 93). Apply the liquid with a watering can to drench the soil at the base of the plants, or spray it on their leaves.

LAWNS

Nothing sets off colorful flowers and handsome shrubs like a lush, green lawn. Good soil preparation is especially important here, as your lawn will be in place for a long time. But with regular applications of compost and a good fertilizing program, even long-established turf can stay in great shape.

Preparing the Soil. When starting a new lawn, take the opportunity to prepare the site well. Even if you never bother with soil tests in other parts of your garden, it's worth testing one or more samples before sowing or sodding. The test results will help you determine if you need to adjust the pH or add nutrients, tasks that are much easier to do *before* installing a lawn.

Start preparing the soil by spreading any needed fertilizers and amendments over the area, then top that with a 1- to 2-inch layer of compost or other organic matter. (If your soil is on the sandy side, or if you live in the South, you'll get longer-

---

Aerating Lawn Areas

Treating your lawn with a core aerator every few years will help keep it in great condition. It will minimize problems due to compaction and will allow water, fertilizer, and topdressings of organic matter to reach grass roots more quickly.

lasting benefits by using a coarser-textured material, such as ground pine bark, either alone or mixed with some compost.) Then turn the fertilizer and organic matter under to thoroughly mix it with your soil. Unless you have a very small lawn, this is one time where it's really most practical to use a rotary tiller: you can cover a lot more ground quickly, and you'll get the best mixing with fewer surface lumps. After tilling, rake the surface to break up any remaining clods and to remove rocks and other debris; then you're ready to sow grass seed or lay sod.

Fertilizing. If your lawn looks healthy and vigorous, a yearly topdressing of compost may be all it needs to stay that way. This is, of course, if you let the clippings fall back onto the lawn when you mow. Otherwise, you're removing an important source of nutrients and organic matter. If you adjust your mowing schedule so you don't remove more than the top third of the grass blades each time, the clippings will be fine enough to fall down through the remaining grass. The only time you should bag or rake the clippings is when you've waited too long to mow and then cut the lawn to its normal height. Piles of large clippings can quickly mat down and smother the grass, so pick them up and add them to your compost pile or use them as mulch in the vegetable garden.

Finished compost is an excellent source of both nutrients and organic matter for a lawn. The material needs to be fairly fine so that it will work down through the grass and not mat down on top of the turf. Screening the compost through a $1/4$- to $1/2$-inch-mesh screen produces a uniform, easy-to-spread material. (See the illustration on page 88 for tips on making a simple compost-sifting screen.) Scatter it by hand over small areas or use a lawn spreader to apply a layer about $1/4$ inch thick. A once-a-year application—in late summer in the North, in spring in the South—provides great results.

If you prefer to use a commercial fertilizer, look for one that has been formulated with organic ingredients. Chemical-based fertilizers are usually less expensive and give a quicker "green-up," but their benefits won't last as long. Not only will you have to mow more often to control the fast growth after fertilizing, the lush growth is more prone to pest and disease problems. Organic fertilizers release their nutrients slowly over a longer period, promoting more even growth and reducing the need to mow or fertilize as often to keep your lawn looking good. Apply the fertilizer according to the recommendations on your soil-test report or follow the

When planting a new lawn, it pays to prepare soil thoroughly to ensure healthy, vigorous turf that's easier to care for. Have the soil tested, then spread the recommended amendments over the lawn and till them in. Installing steppingstones in high-traffic areas will prevent worn spots.

rate suggested on the label. Scatter it by hand over small areas or use a spreader for even coverage on larger lawns. In the North, fertilize in late summer, before your grass goes dormant for the winter; in the South, wait until spring.

Aerating. The soil under lawns is especially susceptible to compaction, as it is subjected to a lot of foot traffic from playing and mowing. Aerating your lawn every few years can dramatically improve rooting conditions, especially in lawns that get a lot of use. Aerating allows more air and water into the soil, minimizes the buildup of thatch (undecomposed clippings and roots), and makes it easier for fertilizers to reach the root zone, where they are needed.

In very small areas, a spading fork will serve the purpose: insert the tines as far as you can, then wiggle the handle back and forth; repeat every 6 inches or so. For best results, though, use a tool with hollow or open tines, which will punch or scoop out some soil and deposit the plugs on the surface. Use a manual aerating tool for small areas (less than $\frac{1}{8}$ acre or so) or rent a core aerating tool for treating larger lawns.

Aerating is easiest when the soil is slightly moist, so do it a day after it rains or after you have irrigated thoroughly. You can leave the plugs on the surface (they'll break down fairly quickly) or rake them up and add them to the compost pile. Add a topdressing of finished compost after aerating to help the organic matter and nutrients get down into the root zone.

SHRUBS, TREES, AND VINES

Of all your plants, shrubs, trees, and woody vines tend to require the least special soil treatment. This doesn't mean that they won't benefit from some extra care, but they will usually do well without it—especially if you select species that are naturally suited to your soil and climate conditions.

Preparing the Soil. These large plants have quite extensive root systems, so it's usually not practical to make extensive changes in your soil to suit their needs. If your soil tends to be soggy, choose shrubs and trees that thrive with wet feet (see "Plants for Wet Places" on page 48) rather than trying to grow roses or other plants that need good drainage. While most shrubs and trees can adapt to a wide pH range, some are better suited than others to acid or alkaline conditions, so consider this too if your soil has a pH lower than about 6.2 or higher than 7.2. (To find out which shrubs, trees, and vines are best suited to your area and type of soil, check with your local Cooperative Extension Service or visit a local arboretum.)

When you are ready to plant, dig a planting hole that is just as deep as the root ball and two to three times wider. Slope the sides of the hole so the top is wider than the base and scratch the sides to loosen the soil. Set your plant in the hole and backfill with the soil you have removed. Years ago, experts used to recommend mixing peat moss or other organic matter into the planting hole. Recently, how-

Mulching Shrubs and Trees

To mulch newly planted—or existing—shrubs and trees and add nutrients to the soil at the same time, start by applying a $^1/_2$- to 1-inch-deep layer of compost in a circle that extends several inches beyond the farthest reach of the branches. Top that with 1 to 2 inches of a coarser, longer-lasting mulch, such as shredded bark or wood chips. Make sure you keep any mulch 4 to 6 inches away from stems or trunks.

ever, that advice has changed, as people noticed that shrubs and trees planted like this often produced roots only in the loose, organic-rich soil in the planting hole, the equivalent of planting in a large container. Eventually, when the roots depleted the moisture and nutrients in the hole, growth suffered. And since the roots didn't penetrate into the surrounding soil, the plant wasn't well anchored and was more likely to blow over in a high wind. For these reasons, it's best to avoid adding any fertilizers or amendments to the soil you return to the planting hole.

If you do want to put some effort into creating excellent rooting conditions for trees or shrubs, consider preparing large planting beds rather than digging individual holes. Use the same techniques you would use to create a new perennial garden (see "Preparing the Soil" for perennials on page 98), spreading organic matter and fertilizers over the whole area and digging or tilling them

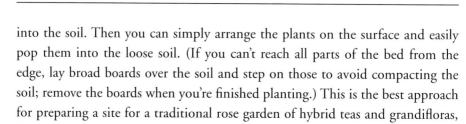

into the soil. Then you can simply arrange the plants on the surface and easily pop them into the loose soil. (If you can't reach all parts of the bed from the edge, lay broad boards over the soil and step on those to avoid compacting the soil; remove the boards when you're finished planting.) This is the best approach for preparing a site for a traditional rose garden of hybrid teas and grandifloras, for example. The new, tough shrub roses can be planted just like other shrubs, as recommended above.

Mulching. Start mulching trees, shrubs, and vines right after planting and watering. Spread compost over the soil in a circle that extends beyond the branches. Then top that with a coarser mulch to help retain moisture and suppress weeds. Keep all mulches away from the base of the stems or trunk. Mulch piled close to the stems holds moisture there, encouraging disease problems. It also provides a home for mice and other pests that chew the softened bark and damage or kill your plants. Add more mulch as needed each year to keep it at the recommended depth.

Fertilizing. Mulching with compost goes a long way toward meeting the nutrient needs of young trees and shrubs. Each spring, rake off the remaining mulch, add another $1/2$- to 1-inch layer of compost, then replace the coarser mulch.

If you want to give your plants an extra nutrient boost, spray their leaves with a dose of liquid fertilizer. Use seaweed (kelp) extract or fish emulsion, diluted according to the label directions, or make your own liquid fertilizer by soaking compost in water (see "Making Compost Tea" on page 93). Of course, this method is practical only with shrubs and small trees. Early summer to midsummer is a good time to apply liquid fertilizer. Avoid fertilizing after midsummer; the extra nutrients can promote a flush of tender new growth that may be damaged by early cold snaps.

If you suspect a shrub or tree is developing a nutrient deficiency (yellowish leaves with green veins are a common sign of iron deficiency, for instance), collect a soil sample near the base of the plant and have it analyzed by a soil-testing lab. The report will indicate if there are any nutrient imbalances and give suggestions for correcting the problem.

Caring for Container Plants

Growing plants in pots adds interest and flexibility to your garden. Containers give you extra growing space for flowers, herbs, and vegetables, and it is easy to rearrange the pots and planters as needed to create attractive displays throughout the season. To keep your potted plants looking their best, though, you'll need to give them a little special attention.

Regular watering is a key part of container care. In the heat of summer, a large pot full of plants may need a gallon or more of water every day. Small plants need less water, but they dry out more quickly, so you may need to check them twice a day; the same goes for window boxes and hanging baskets. Plants in clay pots or other porous planters will lose water faster than those in plastic containers. Placing shallow saucers under the pots can help keep the growing medium moist longer. But if you get a rainy spell, remove the saucers until the weather dries out; if the pots sit in water, the growing medium stays soggy and the roots may rot.

The exact amount of water needed varies widely, depending on the plant, the pot, and the weather. But a good general rule of thumb is to water until you see a bit of moisture seeping out the bottom of the container. Don't let the growing medium dry out completely, as rewetting it can be very difficult. If this does happen, set the pot or basket in a pan or bucket filled with several inches of water and let it soak for a few hours; then remove the container and let it sit in a shady spot for a day or two before returning it to its usual spot.

In large containers and tubs, it's tempting to reuse the potting medium year after year, but replacing it annually is best. Not only are nutrients depleted in used potting medium, but the structure tends to break down as well. Dump used medium onto the compost pile and start next season's container plants in fresh soil. Regular fertilizing is another important part of keeping pots, planters, and baskets in top condition. For more information, see "Fertilizing Container Plants" on page 72.

Photo Credits

Patricia J. Bruno / Positive Images: 24

Karen Bussolini: 53 (Johnsen Design and Planning)

Karen Bussolini / Positive Images: 75

David Cavagnaro: 84

Barbara Ellis: 45, 57 right, 94, 97, 99

Derek Fell: vi–1, 36

Charles Marden Fitch: 66, 111

Margaret Hensel / Positive Images: 29

Jerry Howard / Positive Images: 22

Dency Kane: 5 (Marla Gagnum garden, East Hampton, N.Y.),
     89 bottom (Montrose, Hillsborough, N.C.), 103

Nancy Ondra: 61, 80

Jerry Pavia: 2, 21, 34, 54, 57 left, 89 top

INDEX

Page numbers in italics refer to illustrations.

Titles available in the Taylor's Weekend Gardening Guides series:

Organic Pest and Disease Control	$12.95
Safe and Easy Lawn Care	12.95
Window Boxes	12.95
Attracting Birds and Butterflies	12.95
Water Gardens	12.95
Easy, Practical Pruning	12.95
The Winter Garden	12.95
Backyard Building Projects	12.95
Indoor Gardens	12.95
Plants for Problem Places	12.95
Soil and Composting	12.95
Kitchen Gardens	12.95
The Garden Path	12.95
Easy Plant Propagation	12.95

At your bookstore or by calling 1-800-225-3362

Prices subject to change without notice